PRENTICE-HALL
FOUNDATIONS OF MODERN SOCIOLOGY SERIES

PRENTICE-HALL
FOUNDATIONS OF MODERN SOCIOLOGY SERIES

Alex Inkeles, Editor

THE SCIENTIST'S ROLE IN SOCIETY
Joseph Ben-David

DEVIANCE AND CONTROL
Albert K. Cohen

MODERN ORGANIZATIONS
Amitai Etzioni

SOCIAL PROBLEMS
Amitai Etzioni

LAW AND SOCIETY: An Introduction
Lawrence M. Friedman

THE FAMILY
William J. Goode

SOCIETY AND POPULATION, Second Edition
David M. Heer

WHAT IS SOCIOLOGY? An Introduction to the Discipline and Profession
Alex Inkeles

THE SOCIOLOGY OF SMALL GROUPS
Theodore M. Mills

SOCIAL CHANGE, Second Edition
Wilbert E. Moore

THE SOCIOLOGY OF RELIGION
Thomas F. O'Dea

THE EVOLUTION OF SOCIETIES
Talcott Parsons

RURAL SOCIETY
Irwin T. Sanders

THE AMERICAN SCHOOL: A Sociological Analysis
Patricia C. Sexton

THE SOCIOLOGY OF ECONOMIC LIFE, Second Edition
Neil J. Smelser

FOUNDATIONS OF MODERN SOCIOLOGY
Metta Spencer

SOCIAL STRATIFICATION: The Forms and Functions of Inequality
Melvin M. Tumin

RURAL SOCIETY

RURAL
SOCIETY

IRWIN T. SANDERS

Boston University

Prentice-Hall, Inc., Englewood Cliffs, New Jersey 07632

Library of Congress Cataloging in Publication Data

Sanders, Irwin Taylor (date).
  Rural society.

  Bibliography: p.
  Includes index.
  1. Sociology, Rural. I. Title.
  HT421.S25 1977   301.35   76–30737
  ISBN 0–13–784447–6
  ISBN 0–13–784439–5 pbk.

© 1977 by Prentice-Hall, Inc., Englewood Cliffs, N.J. 07632

Printed in the United States of America

10 9 8 7 6 5 4 3 2 1

Prentice-Hall International, Inc., London
Prentice-Hall of Australia Pty. Limited, Sydney
Prentice-Hall of Canada, Ltd., Toronto
Prentice-Hall of India Private Limited, New Delhi
Prentice-Hall of Japan, Inc., Tokyo
Prentice-Hall of Southeast Asia Pte. Ltd., Singapore
Whitehall Books Limited, Wellington, New Zealand

To my wife
who, in our travels,
visited more out-of-the-way rural communities
than she had bargained for. . . .

CONTENTS

PREFACE

There are several excellent books introducing the reader to the content and methods of rural sociology; there are other valuable books dealing chiefly with the changes in the rural society of the United States. Nevertheless, the justification for a new book on rural society is two-fold. First, any full-fledged treatment of the topic must make the reader aware that rural problems exist on a world-wide scale and that rural life as we know it in the United States is very different from rural life in most nations of the world. In other words, rural sociologists of all people, if they are to deal with rural societies, must shake loose from any remaining parochialism and familiarize themselves with the "rural experience" in other countries. This is why so many illustrations from other continents appear in this volume.

A second justification for this book is the author's belief that he has used a relatively simple scheme—that of social articulation—for dealing with a wide variety of topics in different social settings. It has seemed best to apply one approach systematically, even to the point of repetition, rather than introduce a much more complicated conceptual scheme that could only be inadequately applied in an introductory volume. The purpose of a beginning book on rural society is to present a reasonable amount of material in some orderly perspective in the anticipation that the reader, once informed and interested, can move on to more detailed expositions and more highly elaborated conceptual schemes. This can happen if the initial impact or introduction is solid, consistent, penetrating in places, and provides at least the rudiments for fitting daily news about rural people, from far and near, into some comprehensible (though not necessarily comprehensive) context.

Grateful acknowledgement is made to former graduate students Ann Brownlee, Roger Whitaker, and Willard van Horne for ideas about social articulation; to Alex Inkeles, series editor, for his valuable critiques; and to those who helped prepare the various versions of the manuscript for publication—Johnnie Scott and Laura Willard. Especially, I should express gratitude to rural people in various regions of the United States and in several foreign countries for patiently introducing me to details of their life and the changes they face.

RURAL SOCIETY

CHAPTER 1
THE STUDY OF
A RURAL
SOCIETY

The drama of change in rural societies is now being played on a world-wide stage. Its actors are the agents of change: the political innovators, both revolutionaries and reformers; the educators who bring a vision of a different life to rural children; the public health nurses who sponsor campaigns against age-old practices in order to lengthen the life span; the tractor sales people with their easy credit terms; and the community development specialists who urge barefoot villagers to raise themselves by their own bootstraps. Also on stage are representatives of the so-called "target population," the rural people who are being asked to change their family life (family planning), their farming techniques (scientific agriculture), their religion (new political "saints"), their sense of priorities (migration to the city to work in factories), and—in sum—their total way of life.

In the West, this drama unfolded a century or so ago; elsewhere its acts are today being compressed into a few decades.

An appreciation of the features of a rural society can give those in a modernized nation a better understanding of their recent rural past. It can also explain much about the behavior of the other nations of the world, the majority of whom are still predominantly rural.

WHAT IS A RURAL SOCIETY

Some have argued that all of those engaged in agriculture comprise the members of a rural society. Certainly, such a common *occupational* concern leads to many similar attitudes and social institutions. Today, a more widely accepted definition of "rural" is the *size and density of settlement*. Population aggregates varying from 1,000 to 5,000 are set by different countries as the cut-off points between rural and nonrural.[1]

However defined, most rural people do have a way of life that is different from residents of towns and cities. What is to be the focus in describing these differences?

One can concentrate on the *rural individual* and try to analyze how his attitudes toward work, time, family, community, and religion are woven into his personal behavior and his view of the world: whether he resists or welcomes change; or whether he wants his children to stay on or to leave the farm. Even in the United States the range is broad. The concerns of the Wisconsin dairy farmer who is tied to a herd needing daily care are different than those of the Nebraska farmer who can turn to other things (even fishing in Florida) while he waits for the wheat he has sown to ripen for harvest. The lives of farmers with the irrigated, highly productive vegetable farms of California are in sharp contrast to those of farmers with the unproductive hillside farms of Appalachia. But all of these rural people are part of the larger American society that has given them a common political heritage.

What, then, of the variations between the Pakistani peasant and the Mexican peasant, the Norwegian farmer and the Greek farmer, the newly settled nomad in Saudi Arabia and the rice grower in Japan, or the collectivized farmer of Bulgaria and the African farmer still conscious of tribe and extended family? Since society is made up of its individual members, a focus upon individuals does give much insight into that society; they are its carriers although a society exists beyond the life span of any single individual. But an emphasis only upon the individual leaves out the broader network of social relationships of which he or she is a part.

A focus upon the *rural family* moves one a giant stride ahead in the analysis of a rural society. A family description must be related to a specific rural society since no single family pattern can be termed *the rural family*. In some countries it is highly autocratic, while in others loose-jointed and democratic; the role of the wife and mother may be paramount or played down; the nuclear family of parents and children may be the basic unit of control or only a part of a much larger family system in which the desires of a particular nuclear family may be submerged in the interests of the extended family group. In some societies, land may be allotted to the family by the tribal elders as the family is

1. Olaf Larson, "Rural Society," *International Encyclopedia of the Social Sciences*, Vol. 13, New York: Macmillan, 1968, pp. 580–88.

able to cultivate it; in other places the family seeks to pass on its prized fields from generation to generation. An adequate portrayal of a changing rural society must include the features of the family institution, but the canvas must be broader than family and kin.

The best documented aspect of many rural societies is the *local community*. In it one observes members of the society moving outside the family group into contact with other family groups and with representatives of the other institutionalized systems of the society: government, education, religion, economy, health and welfare, and recreation. In very small communities, these systems may have only rudimentary representation. Those who have responsibility for trying to change agricultural practices or for improving living standards in rural areas have found that the arena of action is usually the local community. The community is an important agency for the formation of individual public opinion for or against some proposed change; it can also provide facilitating services to those who choose to accept the change. Despite its practical importance to change and its multifaceted insight into various features of a rural society, no single rural community fully represents a rural society.

The *rural society* consists of a wide variety of family groups, rural organizations, and institutional complexes, as reflected in communal life. Therefore, rural society is an analytic concept, a piecing together of many types of individual and group behavior. It is an abstraction. One can pick out a farmer, visit his farm, talk to his family, and walk about his community. These are visible, identifiable objects. The overall society to which he belongs is also real, but it cannot be seen as a group of people can be seen. Yet people act as though there were a tangible rural society. Policy planners project schemes for changing agriculture and the customs connected with it; individuals know when they move from a rural to an urban setting; and young people develop aspirations which may keep them rural—since they may want to stay in agriculture and live in a small settlement—or make them urban—since they may seek to escape from the farm. Thus the concept of a rural society proves extremely useful. With industrialization and urbanization the rural segment grows smaller in the society, but the remaining rural people must provide the others with food and fiber,[2] with crops for export, and with a sense of continuity with the past on which new nations must be built.

Concepts drawn from general sociological theory are usually employed to analyze rural society. Some of the more frequent are *status*, *roles, value*, and *norms*. These can be illustrated in the case of a *social relationship*, or a bond (represented by the arrow in Fig. 1–1) between

2. W. K. Warner, "Rural Society in a Post-Industrial Age," *Rural Sociology*, **39** (1974), pp. 306–18.

two social actors (persons, groups, systems), each with a *status* recognized by the actors as well as by others in the system. Connected statuses may be father–son, mother–daughter, politician–voter, merchant–buyer, farmers' cooperative–national bank, and on through hundreds of possibilities. Social structure may actually be viewed as the totality of statuses.

Roles are the dynamic aspect of status, and their combination constitutes the social process. For every status in a given situation there are roles, or behavior patterns, which are considered appropriate and therefore expected. Fathers and sons are supposed to behave toward each other in certain ways under specified circumstances. Having said this, however, we must add that these expected behaviors are frequently modified by the individual actors who do not behave as automatons fashioned by the society.

The common acceptance of values by the actors in a social relationship helps them arrive at a mutual definition of the situation in which they find themselves. Values are also embodiments of social principles: the value of honesty means that merchants and buyers should treat each other in certain ways, but a value such as male supremacy prescribes behavior involving a hierarchy or ranking principle, which, in this case, stipulates that women should be subservient to men. Thus a knowledge of the values helps determine which of the actors is superordinate or subordinate, with a coordinate status occasionally encountered.

Norm refers primarily to role enactment and specifies the rules within which the behavior is to be carried out. We have already mentioned the individual variation encountered in role-playing, but society does set some limits. Although a farmer may drive a neighbor's pig out of his field, he would violate a norm if by using too much force he killed the pig.

The social relationship diagrammed in Figure 1–1 is a building block for networks which combine a number of social relationships connecting congruent statuses (father and son but also mother, daughter,

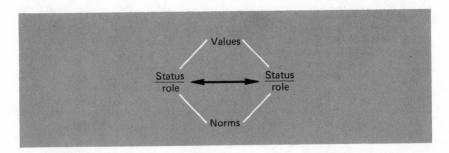

Figure 1-1 A social relationship.

sister, brother, grandfather, aunt). Supposedly in such a network there are shared family values, sufficient agreement about roles, and an understanding of the rules, or norms.

The social network, in the sense used here, refers to the components of a social system that can be *logically* related to each other and they can be presumed to have a real functional connection. (A social network differs from a *personal network*, which traces the social contacts of a particular person through time, or from the *sociometric network*. A sociometric network is based on preferences of individuals for other members within a group in connection with specified tasks or activities. A *sociogram* results when lines are drawn between individuals and their choices.)

Economic subsystems (commerce, transportation, industry, banking, agriculture, etc.), political subsystems (party organization, official ministries or departments, judicial, etc.), as well as subsystems pertaining to educational, recreational, religious, and other major systems are the units or actors in the kind of network used here.

In other words, we start with a conceptual network that can be made specific to the realities of any particular society, recognizing that the actual expressions of these networks will vary in capitalist and socialist societies, in highly industrialized and less industrialized societies, as well as in those where the rural population forms a major proportion of the population in contrast to those societies where it constitutes a small proportion.

The key to understanding this kind of network is the recognition that various people fill the existing statuses, that they have been trained to play the roles connected with these statuses vis-a-vis those occupying related statuses. Such role playing takes place within the context of values and norms already described.

Equipped with these and additional concepts, a rural sociologist is prepared to describe the chief characteristics of any given rural society. However, it is increasingly clear that the assumption that the rural society is isolated often leads to incomplete and even erroneous conclusions. What is needed instead is to learn about some of the significant features of the rural society, but also to note how these are linked with the larger, national society. For that reason, the chief emphasis in succeeding chapters will be upon the process whereby the rural society becomes more closely connected with the larger society. We call this process *social articulation*,[3] and we will make frequent use of the concepts just described.

---

3. Many social scientists have worked on various aspects of social articulation. Illustrative of these are Charles P. Loomis (*Social Systems: Essays on Their Persistence and Change*, Princeton, N.J.: D. Van Nostrand Co., 1960) who analyzes "systemic linkage"; Robert Redfield (*Peasant Society and Culture: An Anthropological Approach to Civilization*, Chicago, University of Chicago Press, 1956) who

SOCIAL ARTICULATION
AS A CENTRAL ORGANIZING THEME

In social science the term *articulation* has come to mean the congruence, or the working together, of parts of a social system. Particularly, as used in this book, it describes *the process by which the rural society becomes incorporated more fully into the larger society while maintaining many of its rural institutions.* In other words, the rural society does not become assimilated in the sense of losing its identity altogether; nor does it become integrated to the point of becoming an indistinguishable part of the whole. Rather, it becomes articulated so that its parts become meshed, linked, related to the social units external to it.

It is important to distinguish among three *indexes of articulation* that indicate the degree to which the rural society (or an aspect of it) has become similar to the national society:

Material Achievements.   One kind of articulation has occurred when rural people share many of the same material culture traits identified with urban or "modern" living. These include better housing, sanitary facilities, suitable clothing, improved nutrition, and more convenient household appliances. The farmers follow scientific agricultural practices as evidenced by new types of seed, new agricultural machinery or implements, rat-resistant storage sheds, and better crop rotations.

Communication provides other indications of material articulation: farm to market roads, radio and television use, newspaper and periodical distribution, and even the extent of personal travel.

Many of these items may appear in carefully-prepared statistical data. These make possible the comparison between two points in time and also between two regions of a country or even between two countries.

Attitudinal Changes.   Rather than concentrating only on material things, we might look at the people themselves, particularly their attitudes. Are the thought processes of rural people still different from those of urban people or are they no longer separable?[4] Rural sociologists have

<hr />

views peasantries as "part-societies"; Arthur J. Vidich and Joseph Bensman (*Small Town in Mass Society: Class, Power and Religion in a Rural Community,* Princeton, N.J.: Princeton University Press, 1968) who deal with "gatekeepers"; Roland L. Warren (*The Community in America,* Chicago: Rand McNally and Co., 1963), who deals with the community's "vertical pattern"; and Howard W. Beers ("Socio-Economic Development and Man-Land Relationships," *Sociologia Ruralis,* Vol. VIII, No. 3–4, 1968) who sees articulation as a matter of "fit" or congruity among elements and actions.

4. F. K. Willits, R. C. Bealer, and D. M. Crider, "The Ecology of Social Traditionalism in a Rural Hinterland," *Rural Sociology,* **39** (1974), pp. 334–49.

made extensive studies of factors associated with the adoption of new farm and home practices. Some of these describe attitudinal changes, sorting out those informants who have moved from the sacred or traditional to the rational or scientific point of view.

Other kinds of surveys and public opinion polls seek to tap attitudinal differences between rural and urban people. Obviously, to the extent that the differences decrease, one might argue that social articulation is taking place.

Such evidence sheds new light on the individual's shift from being a peasant to being a farmer, from being a subject to being a citizen, from being a ruralite to being an urbanite or cosmopolite.

Social Network Linkages. Since the emphasis upon attitudes centers on the individual as the unit of analysis and not upon his social relationships, a third approach to social articulation would be observing over a period of time how rural social networks become connected with and similar to networks outside the rural sector.

In Figure 1–2, the features of a rural network are placed next to an external or nonrural network, showing the linkage between two networks.

Three situations are possible. First, the two systems are completely different. There is no similarity in the statuses. The incumbents in the two networks do not share the same values, would not understand how to carry out the behavior appropriate to the statuses in the other network, and do not have an appreciation for the norms operating within it. Here there is no articulation.

A second situation would be a complete merger through time in the sense that the statuses in the two networks are no longer different when referring to a common life activity; the incumbents share the same values, carry out similar roles when in the same status, and conform to

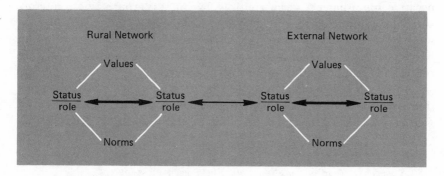

Figure 1-2 Networks in contact.

the same norms. This extreme case has gone beyond articulation to an elimination of one network (assimilation) or the modification of each into a third, new network (amalgamation).

What concerns us here, however, is the third possible situation in which each network maintains its own identity but has developed a congruity with the other in at least some, but not all features. Many illustrations will be given in later chapters of how rural and nonrural networks gain more characteristics typical of the larger society.

COMPETING THEORETICAL APPROACHES

Today, two of the major sociological approaches are the *equilibrium* (social system) and the *conflict* perspectives.[5] The first of these grows out of a social action framework in which society is viewed as if it were a system of interrelated parts. Various parts or components perform functions to meet system needs. Adjustments are continually being made within the system to maintain a moving equilibrium so that it can operate as an on-going entity. Focus is upon the nature of the system, what is needed to keep it in operation, and its interaction with other systems.

The conflict school, influenced by but not exclusively connected with Marxism, sees a society as made up of people (or groups) with unequal access to social and economic resources. Therefore, society is a battleground where those who consider themselves exploited rise up against those who exploit them. The concept of revolution or radical change takes the place of the idea of equilibrium.

A. Eugene Havens has prepared a table which succinctly compares important differences between the equilibrium and conflict approaches as far as the development of a society is concerned.

To summarize, the person looking for equilibrium will be impressed by consensus and common values, by both positive (encouragement) and negative (punishment) social controls, by interest groups whose interdependence reinforces each other. Those looking for conflict will find instances of exploitation, of rising consciousness of their condition by the have-nots, and of signs of actual or impending struggle among those who control and do not control the means of production.

The same theoretical schemes can be applied to the relations between the modernized and developing societies, most of which are rural. Robert Rhodes[6] has pointed out that those following the equilibrium

5. For a fuller discussion of these two approaches see Irwin T. Sanders, *The Community*, Third edition, New York: The Ronald Press, 1975.

6. Ideas presented by Robert Rhodes, University Seminar on Pre-Industrial Areas, Columbia University, October 6, 1970.

Table 1–1   Differences in Assumptions Between the Equilibrium and Conflict Approaches to Development*

APPROACH

Issue	Equilibrium	Conflict
1. Interests	Uniting	Dividing
2. Social relations	Advantageous	Exploitative
3. Social unity	Consensus	Coercion
4. Society	System with needs	Stage for class struggle
5. Nature of man	Requires restraining institutions	Institutions distort basic nature
6. Inequality	Social necessity	Promotes conflict and is unnecessary
7. State	Promotes common good	Instrument of oppression
8. Class	Heuristic device	Social groups with different interests

*Derived from Lenski (1966), Dahrendorf (1958), Van den Berghe (1963), Horton (1967), and Adams (1967).

Source: A. Eugene Havens, "Methodological Issues in the Study of Development," Sociologia Ruralis, 12 (1972), p. 255.

model may tend to see developing societies as societies in transition and modernization as involving transformation of traditional social structures. The conflict theorist may see developing societies as stagnant, post-colonial, and modernization as involving destruction of patterns of dominance and dependence created in the colonial period. Second, in terms of the relation of industrial to non-industrial societies, the equilibrium model sees the relationship as benevolent while the conflict theorist sees it as exploitative. Third, the equilibrium theory views development as an evolutionary process while the conflict approach sees it as the result of class conflict and violence. Lastly, the equilibrium theory sees values and attitudes as causal (making things happen) while the conflict theory sees values as the effect or result of institutional arrangements.

In this book, although some references will be made to the conflict approach, the primary emphasis will be upon the equilibrium, or social-systems model. This is because our major concern will be the process by which the rural society becomes more fully linked to the national society of which it is a part.

CHAPTER 2
THE MAN-LAND RELATIONSHIP
FARMING PATTERNS

An important distinction exists between farming viewed as "a way of life" and as "a way of making a living." In the former, economic factors blend with familial, religious, and social factors and so are not the predominant life concerns, although they obviously are very important. However, in the second view, economic forces are predominant and all other factors are secondary. Commercial agriculture, such as a large truck farm producing vegetables for a nearby city, or a citrus ranch producing fruit for markets throughout the United States, are common examples of the second emphasis.

The family farm, small enough to be managed for the most part by the family owning or operating it, is often cited as a case in which the people involved think of farming as a way of life. This is certainly true of family farms in peasant areas of the world, since the profit motive is subordinate to other considerations such as local prestige and faithfully carrying out important traditions and ceremonies. However, when the peasant family begins to produce primarily for the market, uses machinery, prepares the children for careers outside the village, and buys its food, it is moving toward "modern" agriculture. A subtle psychological shift in perspective occurs and new kinds of social change are ushered in as links are formed with networks outside the rural society.

To understand the change from "farming as a way of life" to "farming as a way of making a living" we must be familiar with the varied nature of agriculture: first, with respect to the range of tasks on a single farm and, second, in terms of the variations found from country to country. For this we turn to a consideration of farming patterns.

A farming pattern represents an economic and socio-cultural adjustment to environmental factors, such as land, water, climate, and location. It is economic in that actual products result from the combination of land, labor, and capital. These products have a material value and are used at home, are exchanged, or are sold, thereby involving the farmer in economic transactions much broader than his locality or region. A farming pattern is also socio-cultural in that it is handed down from one generation to the next. It is a focus for social relationships within and without the family, and it reflects cultural values in the decisions made as part of the pattern.

These farming patterns give important clues as to the nature of a rural society. A first task will be to see their common elements by looking at what farmers do or their occupational role.

WHAT A FARMER DOES

The "farmer" described here is the farm owner or farm manager; yet many of the characteristics also hold for agricultural laborers, sharecroppers, and others caught up in the productive cycle of farm work. Significant common features can be grouped under five major headings:

1. Direct relationship to the land.
2. Labor management.
3. Disposal of farm produce.
4. Productive use of capital.
5. Ancillary tasks.

Direct Relationship to the Land

A farmer does not simply enjoy looking at the land or thinking about investing money in buying up more land; he requires land to make things grow. This need forces several concerns. One is concern for the *productivity of the soil.* The farmer may belong to a society in which it is customary to cultivate a few acres of land for three years and then allow it to go back to bush for 35 years so that its productivity will be restored before it is cleared and used again. He may adhere to a crop rotation system in which after each three-year cycle he follows a soil-depleting crop such as cotton or corn with a soil-building crop such as legumes. He may let a field lie fallow for a year or two. He may follow the practice of spreading animal manure over his fields or, as in the case of some East Asian communities, he may use "night soil," or human waste, to provide needed chemicals. If he is practicing scientific farming he may be using artificial fertilizers in carefully calculated amounts and with a chemical composition selected to suit the needs of his own soil. Whatever the means employed—whether inefficient or highly successful—a farmer must deal with the problem of the quality of the soil.

Then, too, farmers everywhere must decide how to utilize their land: what crops to grow or what animals to raise on their acres. In many peasant societies, tradition tends to dictate what is grown. Even there, however, certain choices have to be made. As one moves from self-subsistent farming to market-centered farming, the decisions grow difficult because a number of factors (such as prices) over which a farmer has no control must be considered in reaching a decision about land utilization. *Water management* constitutes a further consideration in a farmer's relationship to his land. This is obvious in irrigated agriculture, but also relates to storage ponds, or drainage ditches to keep a heavy rainstorm from washing away newly-planted seeds. Some crops demand much more moisture than others and their cultivation must be gauged against the water table present. Animals, too, demand fresh drinking water which must be provided at the least cost of labor.

Working the land also has a *seasonality*. The farmer must have a sense of timing; he must know when the soil and climatic conditions are ready for plowing or planting; he must know when a crop should be harvested or animals moved to a different pasture. There is a "right" time to spread manure, to tie up grape vines, to spray an apple orchard, or to dig potatoes.

Therefore, all farmers, simply because they farm, have to deal directly with their land, though how they treat and use it may differ greatly with different farming patterns.

Labor Management

Farming is hard work. Someone must do the innumerable laborious tasks. In a peasant society, the head of the household tends to cultivate as much land as can be handled by members of his own immediate family, except during peak periods. Some owners of large estates may not do any of the work in the fields themselves, but may rent portions to tenants, who pay cash rent and keep as income profits from what they raise. Other landowners may use share-croppers, who pay no cash but turn over a share of the crop to the landlord, the amount depending upon whether or not the landlord contributed more than the land—seeds, fertilizer, draft power, etc. But the tenant farmer and the sharecropper themselves have to manage the labor that goes into the land for which they have assumed responsibility. In some cases landlords prefer to use wage labor. But sometimes this leads to problems. For instance, serious policy implications arise when commercial farmers in California import unskilled Mexican braceros to keep their labor costs down. Ethical questions develop when the commercial fruitgrowers from Texas to Michigan depend upon migrant laborers to harvest their crop. These workers who follow the season often live under deplorable conditions. This is where the conflict theory, discussed in the last chapter, provides a basis for analyzing the extent of exploitation in the owner-farm worker relationship.

As a manager of labor, however, the farmer must always consider the pros and cons of using mechanical equipment to reduce the time spent by his labor force. If he has some under-utilized labor, should he buy or rent labor-saving machinery, such as a tractor, just to be in style? How much supervision should he give to those working with him?

Therefore, a trait common to all farmers, is their concern with ways to recruit, train, utilize, and supervise helpers on the farm. One form of recruitment is a high birth rate that provides sons and daughters upon whose labor one can count. With mechanization, however, size of the labor force becomes less important. Specialized knowledge becomes more important than muscle. Access to urban social networks becomes a crucial issue.

Disposal of Farm Produce

Marketing requires as intricate skills as maintaining the productivity of the soil, and in many farming systems the farmer is expected to master these skills, too. He must not only know what to sell but when to sell and to whom. He must decide in what form—unprocessed or semiprocessed—to dispose of certain crops and at what prices, as well as whether to deliver the crops himself to some buyer in the town or city rather than have the buyer come to his farm.

The farmer must decide how he will store any unsold produce. In some new bins or barns? He must consider how he will protect the stored crops from insect pests and rodents. He may pay someone else to store his crops in the hope that the prices might rise at a later date and that he can then sell to better advantage.

Experience has also taught the farmer how much to keep for his own use. He must decide whether to save his own seed or buy it commercially. A simple solution for the farmer is to work through a local cooperative on the assumption that a collective enterprise can get better terms than could an individual farmer. Farmers learn, often to their sorrow, that much depends upon the competence of the cooperative managers, many of whom get their position because they have no other job opportunity and need a job or because they are related to one of the major officers.

All around the world, except in the very isolated regions, one hears farmers talking about prices and markets. For many, growing the crops is a much less mysterious process than disposing of them.

Productive Use of Capital

Even the farmer who is relatively self-subsistent has to worry about money in today's world. He has to pay some taxes in cash, or he may have to cover the cost of some important family ceremonial: a father's funeral or a daughter's wedding. As far as his farming operation goes, however, he is increasingly dependent upon outside agencies for his supplies and seed. He may also add to his investment in equipment so that he can handle an income-producing crop more efficiently. Or he may want to acquire more land, or more livestock. In other words, most farming patterns are now dependent on money. Calculations are in terms of the national currency. The farmer's production may be limited by the amount of capital at his disposal.

Acquiring and using capital may be crucial. This means that the farmer must know what economic networks are open to him and the rules for making use of these networks. In the past, the village moneylender was characterized as someone who lends when the farmer is in dire need, has no other recourse, and is ready to agree to any usurious terms. Often this type of borrowing and lending resulted in a crop that was already owed in its entirety before it was even harvested. Credit cooperatives are one of the most widespread forms of rural organizations, chiefly because they help tide a farmer over the time when he needs supplies to the time when he sells his crops.

As described earlier, farming combines the factors of land, labor, and capital. Over the years, the capital investment in equipment and farm buildings alone may equal the value of the land at any given time. This is fixed capital which provides no ready cash but perhaps may serve now and then as collateral for a short-term loan to be used for acquiring fertilizer, animal feed, or seeds.

Thus farmers worry about money. They require seed and supplies at a time dictated by the natural growth cycle. They cannot postpone activity by a few weeks to take advantage of some expected income at a later date. Their capital needs are often immediate. Therefore, money management is part of a farmer's job.

Ancillary Tasks

In addition to the more obvious characteristics of farming mentioned above, there is a wide range of other skills a farmer needs. If he raises livestock he must have some knowledge of animal nutrition, how to treat common ailments, how to assist with calving, and also how to castrate male animals. He must possess some construction skills so that he can build poultry houses, pig pens, storage bins, walls around his yard if he lives in a village, and fences around his field. If he uses animal draft power instead of a tractor, he needs to know how to repair a harness or fix a wagon wheel. If he uses machinery, then he should be able to handle simple mechanical problems without having to go to the repair shop in town.

The farm woman also performs a wide repertory of tasks. In fact, her contribution is major, not ancillary. In developing societies she may be expected to card, spin, and weave in order to produce garments or linen for the family; she may also make soap if the family tries to be largely self-subsistent. She preserves food for the winter through drying, pickling, or canning. In addition, she helps with the animals, works in the fields, processes tobacco or some other cash crop, and bakes bread, prepares meals, and cares for the children and the house. On a family farm the husband and wife are thus much more of a working team than in an urban area where the husband works in one place and the wife somewhere else.

The list of farm tasks could be expanded greatly. They illustrate the many skills a farmer must have if he wants to be relatively independent of specialists (the wheelwright, the village carpenter, the local tailor, etc.), all of whom require money which the farmer may prefer to use in other ways. But the list of tasks also underlines the fact that in today's shrinking world the farmer can no longer remain cut off from resources outside his farm. Through the social contacts which he inevitably has to make to procure what he needs, he and his fellow farmers are inextricably linked with the national society. Social articulation is at work.

This brief introduction to the farmer's round of activities with its stress upon some of the common elements, would be misleading without some consideration of the wide variations in farming patterns around the world.

WORLD-WIDE VARIATIONS IN FARMING PATTERNS

The general comments about the work and responsibility of a farmer and his wife are, of course, subject to many corrections when applied to a particular place and type of farming pattern. Figure 2–1 shows how an economic geographer, Emrys Jones, has classified agricultural economies.

First note the areas of the world where no agriculture is carried on, including parts of Africa, which are too dry, and parts of South America,

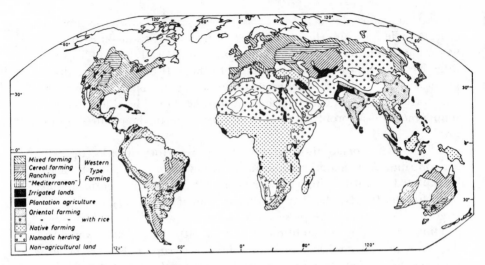

Figure 2–1. Distribution of major agricultural economies.

Source: Emrys Jones, *Human Geography*, New York: Frederick A. Praeger, 1966, p. 103. Reproduced by permission of Praeger and Granada Publishing Ltd., Hertfordshire, England.

where jungle growth is too dense or the mountains too high. Another major differentiation is nomadic herding, which covers much of northern Africa, the Middle East, and Asia.

Native farming, though predominant in tropical Africa, also is found in Central and South America and Southeast Asia. This depends upon shifting cultivation, sometimes called *felling and burning* because the large growth is cut or burned and the ground is then cleared. In Africa, tubers of manioc, yams, or sweet potatoes are placed in holes made by digging sticks; in the New World, maize seeds, along with beans and squashes, are dropped into the holes. In some regions with native (felling and burning) agriculture where hoe culture predominates, the seeds are scattered. But, in any case, after two, three, or four years, the land loses the fertility provided by the ashes from the burned plant growth and the cultivator has to clear new ground and start the cycle over again. With this comparatively inefficient method of agriculture, about 50 acres would be required per family. This assumes that three acres are needed at any one time and that the remainder of the land is not being used, since any patch must rest for 35 years before being brought back into cultivation again.

South and Southeast Asia provide examples of the types of Oriental farming indicated on Figure 2–1. India and Pakistan in particular are areas of dry sedentary farming where climatic conditions are not favorable and where yields were correspondingly low until the recent introduction of new cereal plants able to withstand the harsh environmental conditions. These plants, along with improved farm practices, have led to a "green revolution," which has increased production, though by hardly enough to keep up with the growing population. The wet paddy cultivation in a country such as Thailand is carried out in river valleys and is productive enough to support dense populations.

Western agriculture, usually associated with the temperate zone, has its own interesting variations, including general farming which characterizes so much of Europe and North America. The dairying and corn-hog complex are also part of Western agriculture. Ranching is another part as shown in Figure 2–1. Cereal farming, chiefly wheat, is a widely distributed pattern with a work cycle very different from either dairying or other forms of general farming.

Two other patterns are highly specialized. Irrigation farming usually requires heavy investments in public works so that a large quantity of water is stored and then channeled through a complex system of canals to the fields. As much as any other system, this requires a complex social organization, with a central authority. The other pattern is the plantation which has been characterized not so much as agricultural in the conventional sense but rather as "large-scale, capital-intensive, highly specialized commercial enterprises employing wage labor."[1]

A great variety of farming patterns can be found in a single country. A close look at the United States reveals a dairy region, a cotton belt, a corn belt, a region of corn and winter wheat, a spring wheat region, a hard winter wheat region, a grazing and irrigated crops region, a forestry and pasture region, and subtropical regions in California and Florida. Even these could be further subdivided.

As we have seen, a farming pattern can be described almost entirely in economic terms, if one includes in this the agricultural technology and land utilization. With every farming pattern, however, one finds a sociocultural system which is also part of the total way of life of the farmer, as the following illustration shows.

Peasant Farming in the Colombian Andes: Relatively Self-Subsistent Farmers[2]

Saucío is a small Andean community on a plain in central Colombia. Although Saucío has undergone considerable change, the farming

---

1. Gunnar Myrdal, *Asian Drama: An Inquiry into the Poverty of Nations.* New York: Pantheon, 1966, p. 445.

2. This description is adapted from Orlando Fals-Borda, *Peasant Society in the Colombian Andes: A Sociological Study of Saucío,* Gainesville Fla.: University of Florida Press, 1955.

pattern profiled by Orlando Fals-Borda twenty years ago is useful here as an example of the intensive cultivation of small plots of farmland by traditional methods for subsistence existence.

Ninety percent of the land in Saucío is used to graze cattle or is left idle. Large landowners who own two-thirds of the land account for this use since cattle raising tends to bring them dependable economic returns with only limited inputs of capital or labor and requires relatively little management compared to crop cultivation. The remaining third of the land in Saucío where the majority of resident farmers live, is used almost exclusively for intensive agriculture on predominantly small owner-occupied plots. The plots average only about six acres because of the equal inheritance laws which lead to the generational fragmentation of already small holdings. This remaining third consists of the poorer quality land on slopes which the crop farmers plow vertically. Terrace farming is not practiced.

There are only vague titles and land measurements, so boundaries are imprecise. Simple markers, however, such as rocks, ditches, paths, walls, or creeks prove to be functionally satisfactory to the peasantry. Saucío farmers are described as belonging to the hoe-culture and rudimentary plow-culture stages. Since potatoes are the most important crop grown, the hoe is the most common tool. Farmers also have hand sickles for wheat and barley harvests, axes, shovels, wooden harrows, and wooden plows. The plow is typically a crooked branch with an iron share strapped to the wooden point. Practically all heavy intrafarm transportation is by oxen yoked by their horns. Most transportation of goods to and from markets is done on the heads and backs of the people.

Saucío farmers grow five main crops: potatoes, corn, wheat, barley, and garlic. The economic pivot and the most important staple foods are potatoes and wheat. Potatoes are planted in January or February during the dry season.

Planting potatoes requires five men. The first leads the oxen to trace furrows with the plow. A second man follows and throws the seed into the furrow, usually two tubers in each hole. The next spreads small amounts of manure by hand. The fourth spreads chemical fertilizer, and finally the fifth covers the seed with a hoe.

The potatoes are sprayed three times during the growing season, typically with a rented or borrowed sprayer. Potatoes are harvested in July. This field is then planted, without additional fertilizer, with wheat or barley while a second potato crop is planted elsewhere. Thus there is a short-term rotation system.

Wheat is planted in January or February or in June or July. The wheat field is weeded twice by hand and is harvested in November. Toothed sickles are used to cut the grain which is tied into sheaves by women who use wheat stems as cords and their heads as a catch for the knot. Children then pile the sheaves where they are left to harden for a month. On a sunny, windy day, threshing begins. The farmer rents mules or horses and ties them side-by-side for one radius of the threshing floor. The horses are led around, dehulling the kernels as they step on the wheat. The grain is winnowed by tossing it into the air with wooden spades and forks. The wind carries away the straw and chaff and the grain falls free.

Barley and garlic are grown as secondary crops by the Saucío farmer. Barley is grown for breweries in the larger towns. It is sown and threshed similarly to wheat. Garlic is a dependable crop and needs only one laborer.

Saucío farmers devote relatively large portions of their lots to subsistence farming—to raising crops which are primarily for household consumption. In January or February, they plant various staples simultaneously in land close to the house. Five or six kernels of corn, two of kidney beans, and two of peas are planted together, as are string beans and broad beans. There is little interest among the farmers in vegetable gardening, fruit trees, and cattle fodder.

Agricultural production in Saucío is dangerously low. With poor seed, antiquated planting methods, and inefficient tools, the subsistence existence of the farmer is precarious, yet the balance between production and survival has been maintained by the farming patterns employed by the Saucío cultivator.

But even in this relatively isolated Andean community where hoe culture is practiced, the farmers need to buy commercial fertilizers and pesticides. They need to sell some of their crops to pay for these commercial goods.

The Corn Belt of the United States[3]

Saucío's relatively self-subsistent pattern contrasts markedly with the farm-business in Iowa where conditions are unusually favorable for successful agriculture.

The Corn Belt, centered in the middle Mississippi River Valley, grows about 40 percent of the world's corn. It contains about three-fourths of the 100 million acres in the world that soil technicians rate excellent for grains, grasses, and legumes. Thus, the Corn Belt represents a rare balance of level topography, fertile soil, generous rainfall, and favorable temperatures. The development and spread of hybrid corn in

3. Originally adapted from *The Yearbook of Agriculture*, 1958. Washington, D.C.: U.S. Department of Agriculture.

78-1049

the 1940's led to phenomenal increase in production. Because corn draws heavily upon the fertility of the soil, a Corn Belt farmer rotates other crops such as oats, soybeans, wheat, hay, and pasture crops on about half of his cropland. A corn crop is particularly seasonal in its use of labor and equipment. A variety of crops therefore means that the farmer can distribute his labor more evenly through the growing season: he seeds the oat crop in the spring before work on the corn crop begins and cuts the oats in the summer when cultivation of corn is about over. He plants soybeans, the second most profitable crop in the area after corn, and harvests them earlier. He seeds winter wheat in the fall when the harvest of other crops is mainly over.

Just as the dairy farmer grows hay and small grains to feed to his dairy herd, so the Corn Belt farmer grows corn, a meat-making food, to feed to hogs. About two-thirds of all the hogs in the United States are on Corn Belt farms.

Corn Belt farms also produce from one-fourth to one-third of the poultry in the United States. The poultry, too, are fed corn.

The Corn Belt farmer must be a good businessman. He may have invested as much as $100,000 in a farm averaging just over 200 acres, with the sum depending upon the subregion and quality of soil. He must decide how much corn to grow and, after harvest, how much to sell in terms of his expectations of future prices for corn, hogs, and cattle.

In other words, the Iowa farmer is as much a businessman as an agriculturist.

The Cooperative Farm in Komárov, Czechoslovakia[4]

A far different socio-political system governs farming in Komárov, Czechoslovakia, where in 1955 almost all of the private holdings were aggregated into one large farm managed by a staff of professionally-trained specialists guided by directives from outside their farm. The former owners, who had to turn over all of their land and livestock, and also all their farm machinery, implements, and whatever utility buildings were needed, were put to work for the cooperative which they joined. Some were assigned to crop production, others to livestock production. They were paid on the basis of a production or output norm, which stipulates how much work should be completed in a given time for a specific task. Those families that belong to the farm receive a private plot (maximum 1.24 acres) including garden or orchard. This plot invariably is the object

4.   Adapted from Zdenek Salzmann and Vladimir Scheufler, *Komárov: A Czech Farming Village*, New York: Holt, Rinehart & Winston, 1974.

of great care because it supplies food and some products which the members can sell.

Because of the rural exodus, preferential treatment is now given to cooperative members to relieve the chronic shortage of agricultural manpower. They are now expected to become specialists in various tasks required on the farm and do not have to worry about other aspects of the cooperative for which they have no responsibility. To many, this lifts much of the burden that a farmer cultivating his own fields had to bear. One old villager expressed it this way: "Before the war, when a storm was gathering and clouds were moving toward the village, everyone was running *into* the fields (to take care of animals and crops); nowadays, when people see threatening clouds, they tend to run *from* the fields to home."

FARMING PATTERNS AND SOCIAL ARTICULATION

The preceding pages have dealt with the use of land, how it is worked, and what it produces. Table 2–1 shows that values form an essen-

Table 2–1   Land as a Value in Different Farming Patterns

FARMING PATTERN (Ownership)	VALUE ATTACHED TO LAND	IMPLICATIONS FOR SOCIAL ARTICULATION
1. Felling and burning (Tribally owned)	Usufruct; used and then left idle	Tribal elders reinforce norms; families sell excess produce
2. Hoe culture, self-subsistent (Family owned)	Birthright to be passed on to next generation	Minimal economic contact; extra money put into more land
3. Traditional, labor-intensive (Family owned)	Same as above	Increased economic ties off the farm
4. Mechanized, scientific (Family owned)	Commodity to be bought, sold, or rented as a factor of production	Strong interdependence between farm and economic networks
5. Specialized, large-scale (Corporation owned)	Same as above	Managers have multiple contacts; workers may or may not have labor unions
6. Socialized, state run, either general or specialized (Collectively owned)	A social good; no private ownership	Completely articulated in theory, not always in practice

tial concept in the analysis of social relationships and networks. Land as a social value has different meanings within different farming patterns. Some of these patterns are much closer to the urban-oriented value system, which makes social articulation that much easier. Table 2–1 presents a synoptic though overly-abbreviated illustration of this.

Obviously this is merely suggestive since some types of farming patterns are not included and not all of the possible implications have been spelled out.

The progression from 1 to 6 in Figure 2–1 does not signify any desirability nor inevitability, but it does represent movement from a non-articulated to a much more completely articulated type of farming pattern. Saucío, Colombia illustrates item 2 above; the Corn Belt farmer item 4; and the Komárov cooperative farm item 6.

CHAPTER 3
THE MAN-LAND
RELATIONSHIP
SETTLEMENT PATTERNS

In the articulation process not only do individuals and farms become linked with nonrural networks, but settlements (communities) as units also become connected with each other and with larger urban centers.

The settlement pattern, one aspect of the man–land relationship which intervenes between the natural environment and the social structure, has been defined as "the physical disposition of a population and its segments, its dwellings, other buildings and physical structures related to its social life, on a landscape."[1]

Therefore, a rural settlement, whether high on a hillside or sprawling on a plain, is a form of adaptation to both natural and social conditions. Where land is scarce, the houses are built on poorer rather than better soil; where rivers flood, the dwellings must be out of the way of rising water; where water is difficult to find, the settlement must cluster around existing wells or springs. Some settlements in hilly or mountainous areas strike a fine balance between access to forest products and to pasture on slopes above and the fertile land lying below.

Social considerations also play a part in the location and form that the settlement takes, particularly where security is a matter of some importance and where the walls surrounding the settlement provide a margin of safety. Once started, settlement patterns may continue

1. Ralph W. Nicholas, "Economics of Family Types in Two West Bengal Villages," Seven Articles on Village Conditions, Michigan State University, Asian Studies Center, Reprint Series No. 1, 1965–66, p. 44.

through generations because people have become accustomed to recreational pursuits in a coffee shop or tea house, the proximity of a church or shrine, or the convenience of a small grocery store. The original reason for living together in a compact settlement—namely, safety—may no longer pertain but the social usages continue.

Types of Settlement Patterns[2]

The simplest scheme for classifying settlements is to divide them into the *dispersed* and the *compact*. But having said this, one must begin to describe the many variations within these two types.

The origins of settlement patterns in the United States show two broad variations. In New England, the early settlers tended to form village communities that reproduced as fully as possible the institutions and amenities which the settlers had known in England. In the Southern colonies, however, the newcomers were much more interested in obtaining land for themselves than in creating communities. Isolated farmsteads were set up as soon as the threat of Indian attacks abated. This second pattern prevailed in the opening of the West. The Federal government surveyed an area before it was opened for settlement, dividing a square of six miles into 36 townships, thus creating the familiar grid pattern of roads and fields. Those obtaining title to a section of farmland were required to settle on that land. At first, settling may have meant simply putting up a sod hut or a log cabin, but it did signify residence and the intent to remain.

In other countries, as well, the dispersed community is found. Though the farm residences are some distance apart, there are nevertheless common institutions which the people from an area share and which help give them some feeling of "community" similar to that found in more compact settlements. These "open country communities" have been extensively studied by United States rural sociologists and, before rapid transportation became common, had a distinct social life of their own, with a church, school, a few stores, and a machinery shop as the focal points for social interaction.

A very common type of compact settlement is the nucleated village, which has a genuine center with a series of roads or lanes radiating outward. Often the lanes lose themselves at the edge of the village in land set aside for garden plots; some continue as narrow roads winding through the fields, while others emerge as intervillage roads that the local

---

2. For an excellent treatment of this topic see T. Lynn Smith and Paul E. Zopf, Jr., *Principles of Inductive Rural Sociology*. Philadelphia: F. A. Davis Company, 1970, Chap. 5.

people use on their way to market, or to the "outside world." Rural Austria, for instance, is still characterized by small, largely self-sufficient farm villages heavily dependent upon agriculture and forestry. Although dispersed farmsteads may be found, a majority of the peasant farmers reside in villages scattered along the picturesque mountain valleys and among the foothills of the Alps.[3]

Another type of the compact or agglomerative village is often called the *line village*, although other terminology is employed to describe the fact that the houses are strung out along a main highway or waterway. Only very few houses are built away from this artery since the fields that the villagers own lie behind the houses, extending to the end of the village boundaries. Sometimes these line villages, as in parts of Yugoslavia, stretch for miles, with one fading into another so that the passerby is not aware that he has shifted from one commune or settlement to another. Here, too, there is a central focus for the village, but those on the edge are much farther from it than they would be if they lived in a nucleated village of the same population size.

An additional variation in settlement patterns is the planned rural community. These are created when some new area is reclaimed for agriculture or opened up with the construction of a dam that stores water for irrigation as well as waterpower. The *kibbutzim* in Israel are further examples, since these are set up as completely communal settlements where the planned life is accepted as a matter of course. In the United States, the Mormon village, with its church and social hall, tended to follow a set plan, though it had to adapt to the terrain and to the number of people the land would support.

THE TRADE CENTER-MARKET TOWN

In the United States, with the expansion of the railroads westward, small settlements that later became the trade centers or market towns sprang up. These consisted of a water tower and station, several storage silos in grain-growing regions, and a Main Street paralleling the tracks. In fact, these trade centers performed the function of linking the dispersed farmsteads, so common in their region, with the commercial market beyond. But even so, because of the scattered dwellings and reliance on the rural neighborhood, not many farm people became active in the political affairs or other activities of these trade centers.

In rural areas of the United States today, farm people often flock

---

3. Marvin J. Taves and Hedwig Hönigschmied, "Rural Life in Austria," *Rural Sociology*, **27** (June 1962), p. 199.

to town on Saturdays to do their purchasing, attend the movie or some sports event, and visit with acquaintances. This Saturday phenomenon is so noticeable that local residents of these trade centers, which are often county seats, say that the crowds prevent their going out on this day. Improved transportation and more frequent contacts in the center are making the once-a-week family expedition to the center less important in some more-developed areas.

The market towns of Europe, Asia, and many parts of Africa existed long before the opening up of the New World. Their functions have proven essential for the operation of even the least commercialized farming patterns. The periodic market is held at a set time (same day of the week, for example) in a central place. Producers (farmers or their wives) take what they have to sell to this place and buyers come to haggle for the best possible price. Once the farmer has sold what he brought, he is free to see his rural acquaintances also at the market and even enjoy some of the recreational aspects that are available. At the market he picks up gossip and rumors, comes into contact with outsiders, and forms a general picture of what small producers often speak of as "the outside world." Such a market usually draws farmers from an area that can be covered conveniently by foot or by slow-moving ox-cart, though the traders or buyers may come from a greater distance. These markets resemble the fairs of the Middle Ages. Not only are there stands where farm produce is displayed and sold, but hawkers or petty merchants provide whatever merchandise they think the farmer would like to buy.

Such a market, though colorful and a source of recreation to the farmer, often works to his economic disadvantage. He may set too low a price since he is in competition with other farmers, none of whom is apt to know the actual prices in the urban center to which the farm products go. Furthermore, the trader is ready to take advantage of the fact that the farmer may sell at a lower figure than he anticipated simply because he does not want to transport the calf or the produce all the way back home; or, the farmer may actually have to take whatever cash he can get to make a much-needed purchase, such as medicine or a new plow share, for his family or farm.

Even such a simple approach to marketing as this periodic arrangement involves the farmer in a social network much broader than his village. He gets to talk with relatives and acquaintances from other villages. He deals with the supervisors or organizers of the market who may charge him a small fee for the right to sell. He forms intermittent contacts with buyers and tries to develop effective ways of dealing with them. In other words, he tries to operate as a "trader" in addition to being a farmer, for which different skills are required.

In Nigeria, for instance, most farmers are involved in some sort of trade which may even include nonagricultural products. They have to go to market frequently because they produce on such a small scale and have so little capital that they cannot afford to hold their produce until it is a sizeable amount or to store their produce in suitable facilities. If they do not take the products to market themselves, they dispose of them to a large number of intermediaries using donkey or bicycle transport.

THE IMPORTANCE OF ROADS

Transportation routes represent another form of man's adjustment to the land or natural setting, and they are intimately connected with the development of human population centers. Farm-to-market roads, for instance, provide a means for social articulation. Two cases taken from the author's field work in Greece illustrate this point.

A road, built to open up a large forest area, had passed through Tsepelovo, a village which had seen its first automobile only a few months earlier. When asked what effects the road had had upon the village way of life, the village secretary pointed out first of all the reduced transportation costs, for the hauling charges per oka (2.8 pounds) by truck were only one-fifth or one-fourth of those by donkey. He added:

> Now we can build homes with sand and cement; formerly it was too expensive to carry these in by animals. Formerly we built our stone houses with lime and mud as mortar, and that is why they tend to crumble so quickly. Here we produce about 14,000 okas (about 20 tons) of walnuts each year. We received little for them because of the transportation charges; now the merchant comes here in a truck and pays us cash and gives a higher price. Today we can also sell our lumber because, before the road came, we couldn't very well strap long boards to the donkeys.
>
> We used to spend twelve-and-a-half hours going by animal to Ioannina, the only large city nearby. Now we do it in two-and-a-half hours by car. The grocer can sell fresh goods, whereas formerly he had only staples. Although we had great riches here, we also had great poverty so that beggars would go from house to house. The road reduces this inequality. Many of our men who had no other income earned much money working on the construction.
>
> In case we get sick we can be carried down by car and not have to ride a donkey. Now we can get the Athens newspapers on the same day they are published, whereas before they would always be at least two days late and frequently more. We have no illiterates here, so many subscribe to these papers.[4]

In a village in another part of Greece, where the road had come

---

4. Irwin T. Sanders, *Rainbow in the Rock: The People of Rural Greece.* Cambridge, Mass.: Harvard University Press, 1962, pp. 46–47.

ten years earlier, people well remembered the difference it had made in their lives. One villager compared his village with one without a road:

> The road brought many economic changes. For instance, my father had three hundred cherry trees which he had never bothered to fence in, prune, or tend in any way. Anybody could come and eat the fruit; they would break the branches. But when the road was built, my father fenced in the land and sold the cherries. The income began coming in. Also, it was a disgrace in our village to sell a chicken, but when the road came the women began to sell both eggs and chickens. This meant more income. Eggs in the village without a road sell for half the price obtained by the women in my village. This holds true for all products.
>
> In the village without a road you would have a hard time finding a man with enough cash to buy a candle to light in church, while in my village people always seem to have some cash. In the other village each farmer needs a donkey for transportation and will spend about two thousand drachmas a year just for the upkeep of the donkey; in our village we do not need donkeys because we can use the trucks at much less expense.
>
> Politically, too, roads make a difference. The candidates for parliament seldom get to the villages off the road but try to visit the rest; the same holds true for government officials in position to help in agriculture or other ways. They stick pretty much to the villages which they can easily reach.[5]

To summarize, roads that come to the village squares or near the dispersed farmsteads bring in new services, new ideas, better teachers, and increased economic opportunities, all of which are important to the articulation process. As some express it: "The new road makes us feel we have moved out of the shadow into the sunlight," a psychological dimension which should not be minimized. In the United States, where there is approximately one car for every two Americans, social space is not nearly so restricted as elsewhere. Likewise, the ability to overcome distance easily creates high mobility and leads to an urban-rural mix called the *rural-urban fringe*.

The penetration of the city into rural areas, beyond the suburban zone, brings urban-oriented people into close contact with the rural people who have been living in the area to which the outside urbanites have moved. Good roads and automobiles make it possible for those working in the city or in city-related occupations to travel 30–40 miles each way to work. Although several definitions of the fringe area have been used, its fundamental aspect is that it is an area in transition. It is moving from rural to urban in land use, occupational structure, and social organization. "What is fringe today is most often city or suburb tomorrow." As Fuguitt has noted:

---

5. Ibid., p. 47.

The settlement patterns of fringe areas are usually characterized by scattered nonfarm development. If the area is in farms, there may be an irregular transition from farm to nonfarm land use as some farmers sell off a few lots piecemeal or sell out entirely, while others continue to farm. Sometimes ribbon-like developments along major highways come into being. Thus the city does not usually grow into the rural areas smoothly, but by a "leap-frog" process. It is this scattered development which gives the fringe its peculiar rural-urban character.[6]

ARTICULATION OF THE LOCAL COMMUNITY TO LARGER CENTERS

Just as the individual farmer through various networks becomes linked with the larger society, so the rural community becomes bound to other settlements of varying size through a hierarchy of specialized services.

Hierarchy Among Service Centers

Goods and services related to agriculture appear in even the smallest communities. But these are dependent, in turn, upon larger centers such as the market town, the government administrative center, or even the nearest city. Rural sociologists and social geographers have long been interested in the relationship between size (population) of a community and the services it provides and, particularly, what happens as rural communities lose population and as rural people become more mobile. One analytical development in this regard has been the *central place* approach. This theory holds that population centers may be placed hierarchically and that different levels of the hierarchy may be related to size of place and types of services offered in that place.[7]

Frequency of Types of Service

Another interesting question has to do with the variations in types of service found most frequently. The services in a Spanish village will certainly vary in numerous ways from those found in a small Illinois community. For example, in rural communities of central Illinois, one finds grain elevators and lumber, hardware, and grocery stores but not a single olive press, common in rural parts of Spain. After studying 116

6. Glenn V. Fuguitt, "The Rural-Urban Fringe," *1962 Proceedings of American Country Life Association,* Chicago, Ill.

7. W. Christaller, "Central Places in Southern Germany," *The Pioneer Work in Theoretical Geography,* Englewood Cliffs, N.J.: Prentice-Hall, 1966.

of these Illinois communities, Warren R. Harden drew the following conclusions:

1. Professional people appear on the whole only in the larger communities.

2. Commercialized recreation makes its appearance in the larger communities, providing we exclude the ubiquitous tavern.

3. Where style and fashion are important considerations in a product, the product appears only in the upper range of communities; for example, women's street clothing and men's dress clothing.

4. The more standardized a product is, the more likely it is to appear in the smallest communities.

5. High profit per unit items with low volume turnover tend to appear only in the larger communities, for example, furniture, musical instruments, and carpeting.

6. The more specialized in use a good or service is, the less likely it will appear early in the smaller communities.[8]

He concludes that population and goods and services increase together, thus tending to support central place theory. Conversely, in high population areas which are well organized, especially with respect to transportation and communication, distance may no longer be as important a factor as one would suspect.

Through a method known as a Guttman scale investigators are often able to predict a pattern of services from the knowledge of a single item. An illustration of this is a study of 24 rural Mexican villages in which Frank and Ruth Young have developed a scale of institutional levels.[9] They see these as indicating a single sequence and direction of community articulation with the larger society. The steps in this sequence are the following, with the number in parentheses indicating the percentage of the villages having the listed item (or items):

Step 1. Named and autonomous locality group (100)

Step 2. One or more governmentally designated officials, more than one street (92)

Step 3. One or more organization in village (88)

Step 4. A church (84)

Step 5. A school building, a governmental organization, an *ejido,* mass said in the village more than annually (80)

8.   Warren R. Harden, "Social and Economic Effects of Community Size," *Rural Sociology,* **25** (June 1960), p. 207.

9.   Frank W. and Ruth C. Young, "The Sequence and Direction of Community Growth: A Cross-Cultural Generalization," *Rural Sociology,* **23** (December 1962), pp. 374–86. Also see Eileen A. Maynard, "Patterns of Community Service Development in Selected Communities of the Mantaro Valley, Peru," *Socio-Economic Development of Andean Communities, Report No. 3,* Cornell Peru Project, Department of Anthropology, Cornell University, 1964.

Step 6. A functional school (76)

Step 7. Access to a railroad or informant voluntarily includes railroad in list of village needs (63)

Step 8. Access to electric power, informant estimates that majority have electricity, six or more streets (46)

Step 9. Railroad station, four or more bus or train trips daily (41)

Step 10. School has four or more grades (37)

Step 11. Village has a public square, village market patronized by people in other villages (29)

Step 12. Doctor, priest resides in village, ten or more streets, school has six or more grades, six or more stores, two or more television sets in village, public monument (20)

Step 13. Has one or more telephones (16)

Step 14. Forty percent or more have radios, settlement area one square mile or more (12)

Step 15. Secondary school, twenty or more stores (8)

A later study concerning the institutional complexity of Mexican villages showed that all but two of these items scaled as they had in the Youngs' study. Step 10 had to be changed to "School has six or more grades" and Step 14 had to be dropped since everybody had radios in 1966.[10]

A comparison between Colorado and Sweden also shows the unidimensional hierarchy of services in each place. But there were great differences in relative order of services between Colorado and Sweden because of different factors operating in the two locales.[11]

A theory of social articulation, as the above examples have shown, must take into account the fact that various communities as service centers are in competition with each other. Obviously, while some gain services, others lose them. As the services disappear in a given settlement, people there have to do without or, as is more likely, move farther afield to other places to satisfy their needs. This impersonal economic process, related to population growth as well as ease of mobility, is an important force in connecting the rural segment more closely to the larger national society. The communities that are economically more viable, introducing increasing services from outside, bring about interdependence; in the communities which are economically less viable, the people themselves must make contacts outside if they are to procure wanted services. In this way they become linked—economically at least—to larger centers.

10. John J. Poggie, Jr. and Frank C. Miller, "Contact, Change and Industrialization in a Network of Mexican Villages," *Human Organization*, 28 (Fall 1969), p. 192.

11. Jules J. Wanderer and George R. Smart, "The Structure of Service Institutions in Rural and Urban Communities of Colorado and Sweden," *Rural Sociology*, **34** (September 1969): 3, pp. 368–74.

CHAPTER 4
ECONOMIC NETWORKS IN MODERNIZING AGRICULTURE

A more complete picture of rural society requires a treatment not only of *man–land* but also of *man–man* relationships. Such a shift leads us to the study of the major systems of the larger society, such as the economy, of which agriculture is a major subsystem. The sociological topic to be raised in this chapter is the way in which economic networks, such as those found in the financial or commercial subsystems, link those in the agricultural networks to the rest of their society. Before doing this, however, we must deal with agricultural modernization itself.

THE QUESTION OF AGRICULTURAL MODERNIZATION

"Traditional" versus "Modern"

Changing the traditional patterns to the point that most people accept and encourage the application of the scientific method to farming is often called *modernizing* agriculture. Ness has contrasted traditional and modern societies in which agricultural patterns are quite different:

> By traditional we normally mean that most people in a given population are organized into small and isolated groups in rural areas; they consume most of what they produce and produce most of what they consume in essentially subsistence economies; their work is largely agricultural with a related set

of activities essentially derived from their agricultural production; they are connected with one another as specific persons with a highly diffuse set of obligations and claims upon one another; and by and large they experience a low level of welfare, marked by high morbidity and mortality.[1]

He sees the opposite characteristics in a modern society:

... Most people in a given population are organized in larger collectivities with a great deal of literate communication and interaction with a large and ever growing community, and they live more in urban areas than in rural areas; they sell most of what they produce and buy most of what they consume in highly complex and extensively commercialized economies; they work in factories with machines, and in a wide range of highly specified services; they are related with one another largely on the basis of limited interchanges in which obligations and claims are tied to specific performances or roles rather than to specific persons; and by and large they have high levels of welfare, marked by low morbidity and mortality.[2]

Although such a comparison is presented as an objective statement of fact, few terms such as modernization have a neutral meaning. To apply this term to a given country may give the impression that a "giving" culture is passing judgment upon a "receiving" country as being inferior, backward. This happens even though one tries to define the terms with references to technological advancement but with no intent to pass judgment upon the other aspects of the country's way of life. Some people are concerned that any involvement by an "advanced" country in the modernization of another country introduces a dependent relationship, which might be construed as exploitation by the advanced country. Under certain circumstances, such involvement is described as *colonialism* or *imperialism*, particularly by critics of the Western World. Without doubt, the nations of the Third World need the assistance of those countries with the most technological and economic resources, but no way has yet been found to avoid the likelihood of a dependent relationship in the foreseeable future.

An Innovative Agricultural Technology

Modern agriculture requires an innovative technology, which systematically adapts scientific knowledge to farming. Some of its characteristics are the replacement of a less efficient machine by a more efficient machine, the introduction of new crop varieties, the organization of the distribution of improved seeds, the utilization of new chemical inputs

1. Gayl D. Ness (ed.), *The Sociology of Economic Development: A Reader*, New York: Harper & Row, 1970, p. 6.

2. *Ibid.*, p. 7.

such as herbicides and pesticides, the development of new systems of animal nutrition, and the fostering of package-of-practices principle in which farmers adopt integrated systems made up of several related practices as a substitute for single-factor innovation.[3]

There are many indicators measuring technological change, such as the investment per worker. In the United States between 1940 and 1966 the average value of assets per farm worker increased from approximately $3,000 to $46,000, with the value of land included as an asset. Another indicator is the number of persons each farm worker supplied with farm products. In 1900 it was 7.0 persons, including the farmer himself; in 1940 the figure increased to 10.7, and in 1967 to 42.5 persons.

Some of the effects of such technological change in rural United States have been the following:

> The average size of farms has increased greatly over the years and production has tended to be concentrated in large farms.
> Compared to farms of the past, most farms today are already specialized units and are easily labeled. They are cash grain, corn-hog, fruit, dairy, etc. . . . Farm employees are increasingly being hired for specialized roles.
> . . . Management has become increasingly complex and important. . . . In the future farmers may be assisted in making the key decisions by computers and management services.[4]

Other possible effects now under study by rural sociologists are loss of autonomy by farmers, increase in level of living, expanded leisure, and alienation of the farm employee. In addition, rural sociologists are studying the effect of increased farm size upon the viability of local community services, community differentiation, population size and composition, affluence, and pluralism.

Some conclusions drawn from a study of nine European countries and the United States (Louisiana) show that mechanization may lead to cooperation among farmers in the use of machines. It may lighten physical burdens but cause much worry about covering the financial investment in machines. Additionally, it may lead to frustration among farmers if they cannot enlarge their farm units to take advantage of the machinery they have.[5]

3. Howard W. Beers, "Socio-Economic Development and Man–Land Relationships," *Sociologia Ruralis*, **8** (1968): 3–4. Special Issue, pp. 343–44.

4. Jerry D. Stockdale, "Social Implications of Technological Change in Agriculture," a paper presented at the annual meeting of The Rural Sociological Society, August 29, 1969, p. 6.

5. U.S. Department of Agriculture, *Changes in Agriculture in 26 Developing Nations: 1948 to 1963*. Washington, D.C.: Foreign Agricultural Economic Report No. 27. Economic Research Service. November 1965, p. 109.

The societal changes also deserve much fuller study. For instance, changing technology in the Cotton South brought about the displacement of unskilled workers, adding to the ghetto problems of Northern cities which received these workers as migrants. Another matter of great concern is the role of chemical pesticides used in agriculture in changing the environmental quality.

As a reminder that changing technology is connected with dynamic changes in human behavior, we might note its effect in a village on Taiwan:

> The general social effect of these programs has been that when there are significant changes in technology, or new things concerning the cultivation of the farm and the conduct of daily life, a new liveliness occurs in the social relations of the people in a rural community. When the village life is conventional and work on the farm is routine, most of the farmers toil separately and independently, each on one's own farm with his back bent, head down, eyes fixed on the crop: a typical isolationist. The social life he has is limited in his home with his family members. He has very little to do with his neighbors, except in the evenings and on emergency occasions. The social atmosphere in the community stands still and there is almost no social gathering for business discussions or for talking about problems, needs, improvements, etc., in the community. . . .
>
> But when a new and better crop is introduced into the community, when one of the farmers has the courage to plant it, and at the end he reaps a harvest which is much greater than that produced by the old variety, the new wonder will soon have a social effect. . . . Talks and exchange of information and opinions on the subject start among the concerned farmers. . . .
>
> If the introduction of one change, or one new thing, into the farm village has such a social effect as described above, the continuous introduction of many changes, or many new things, would certainly be able to introduce a high degree of dynamism into a rural community.[6]

This case illustrates the movement from the traditional to a modern society and the role of improved agriciultural technology in bringing this about.

ECONOMIC INFRASTRUCTURES
AS LINKING MECHANISMS

In a sociological sense, any economic infrastructure involves social networks. People carrying out different functions have to interact with

6. Martin M. C. Yang, "Social Implications of Action Programs," *Sociologia Ruralis*, **8** (1968): 3–4. Special Issue, pp. 395–96. Also see *Taiwan's Agricultural Development: Its Relevance for Developing Countries Today.* Foreign Agricultural Economic Report No. 39, Economic Research Service, U.S. Department of Agriculture, Washington, D.C., 1968.

one other in order for the economic need to be met. Mention was made in the discussion of the market town in the previous chapter of the problems farmers face in disposing of their produce. In the more traditional societies, the networks are relatively simple since there is usually direct exchange for other products or money.[7] As the standard of living rises, particularly in urban areas, demands for better quality also rise, which means that the farmer is caught up in the marketing network in a way previous generations never thought possible. The roles, or behavior patterns, connected with being a farmer become more numerous and complex. In the first place, he may be urged by the government or by a prospective buyer to produce certain crops or animals, even though he himself might prefer to do otherwise. He may even be furnished seed or breeding stock so that the buyer can be assured of a higher quality product.

One aim of the buyer, of course, is to arrive at a standardized product that can be advertised and distributed with the assurance that the purchaser will receive what he expected. Along with standardization goes both inspection and grading. The farmer may be visited by the buyer's agents at various times to see how the product is coming along, whether proper techniques are being followed. Once the product is ready for delivery, the farmer may be expected to grade or sort it in keeping with standards set as to size, color, firmness, etc. Certain kinds of packaging or processing may be required of the farmer before delivery. The point to be made is that marketing in "modern" agriculture does not simply mean growing something and then selling it to the highest bidder. It means actual involvement with the prospective buyer throughout the whole production process. This is an operating network in which the buyer is susceptible to the pressures of his customers, whether commission merchants, wholesalers, or housewives and in the face of which he may try to influence the farmers' behavior. Complicating the picture, too, is the negotiations about prices, delivery dates, storage, insurance, and credit, as well as time and method of payment. Other actors in the network may be the health inspector, especially in the case of a dairy

7. The literature on rural markets and marketing institutions is immense. See, for instance, "Marketing Institutions and Services for Developing Agriculture," A Seminar Report. Agricultural Development Council, Inc., New York, 1974; William F. White and Lawrence K. Williams, *Toward an Integrated Theory of Development: Economic and Noneconomic Variables in Rural Development*, New York School of Industrial and Labor Relations, Cornell University, Ithaca. ILR Paperback No. 5, February 1968. Section on "Linking the Village to Urban Markets"; G. William Skinner, "Marketing and Social Structure in Rural China," *Journal of Asian Studies*, **24** (November 1964), pp. 3–43; Kelly Harrison and Kenneth Shwedel, "Marketing Problems Associated with Small Farm Agriculture," A Seminar Report. Agricultural Development Council, Inc., New York, November 1974.

farm, or the veterinarian at the threat of a swine virus, or the official from the state department of agriculture carrying out some regulatory responsibility. The shift in and addition to the role repertoire of the farmer illustrates the linkage between the rural producing network and the marketing network.

The credit network also has its linkage features. Though sometimes closely tied with marketing, it nevertheless exists as a distinguishable part of the infrastructure. As in the case of marketing, the credit institution may make certain demands upon the farmer concerning what he grows and how he grows it, thus modifying his role. However, it is in the case of norms that credit networks often seem to cause the most difficulty to farmers not yet fully linked with the economy of the country. The norms relate to rules governing use of credit and its repayment as well as to the sanctions or punishments for violation of the rules. What the farmer who is inexperienced in urban ways may consider to be justifiable reasons for deferring payment may not be acceptable to those extending credit. He may be relying upon personal consideration, as would often be the case in a rural community, but he finds that the credit agency is applying universal norms which fail to take his particular situation into account. This is not to imply that all credit agencies or banks are heartless or impersonal, but rather that they are in turn parts of the larger credit network which is making demands upon them, a fact which may be hard for some farmers to understand. If one of the essentials of modern agriculture is access to credit on reasonable terms, then the farmer using that network needs to learn its characteristic ways and regulations. In some peasant societies, loans from the agricultural bank may constitute the most crucial and worrisome form of linkage with the nonrural world.

Modern farming also requires a supply network. Some businesses or government agencies must take on the responsibility of providing all kinds of supplies to the farmer at a time he needs it. Supplies, to be effectively used, must also be adapted to the needs of a particular farm. This often requires that the farmer seek advice on the right product to buy, thus putting him in a special relationship to the dealer who may give him this advice, or to a county agent or an agricultural officer, whose job it is to provide competent technical information. It may be suggested to the farmer that samples of the soil be sent off for analysis so that the choice of fertilizer may be properly made; he may be told what types of seed resist the pests or diseases of his area or are adapted to the length of the growing season; or the advice may be about which equipment can least expensively carry out some of the farming operations. Without such advice, the farmer would go through a costly trial and error period, an adventure he cannot usually afford with his limited capital.

A further step toward articulation occurs when the farmer or members of his family attend short courses offered by nearby institutes or colleges. Here they learn about the wise selection of supplies and their use.

Little imagination is required to see the shift from traditional agriculture that occurs when farmers become more dependent upon agencies outside the village—not only for marketing, but for the purchase of a wide variety of goods without which they cannot farm profitably.

FARMERS' COOPERATIVES
AS LINKING MECHANISMS

Farmers' cooperatives have become an important feature of agriculture in most countries of the world. Most of them are based on principles developed in Rochdale, England, by a group of English textile workers who founded The Rochdale Co-operative Store in 1840. One principle was "one man, one vote," which differed from a business corporation where voting is on the basis of the amount of stock held. A second principle was that as a nonprofit organization it does not return any profits or savings to the holders of capital but pays interest on the capital it needs. A third principle was that instead of going to those contributing capital, earnings are distributed to patrons on the basis of the amount of business they have brought to the cooperative.

Distinctions are drawn between producers' cooperatives, of which marketing is one type;[8] consumers' cooperatives such as a cooperative store; and service cooperatives, such as a rural electrification cooperative. There is a tendency for them to merge into a general purpose cooperative if the marketing cooperative also undertakes to procure supplies for its members, or even to supply credit until the crop is marketed.

Some cooperatives are local, made up of individual farmers, serving a shipping point or trading center. Each local association is controlled by its own members, who share in the management through membership meetings and through electing boards of directors. Local cooperatives may be members of a federation through an elected board, with individual farmers as indirect members.[9] Regional Cooperatives may cover several counties or parts of several states.

8. Producers' cooperatives (sometimes called *collective farms*) in socialist East European countries are described in the next chapter.

9. Joseph G. Knapp and Anne L. Gessner, "Farmer Cooperatives Today," in *After a Hundred Years: The Yearbook of Agriculture 1962.* Washington, D.C.: U.S. Department of Agriculture. This and the following paragraph adapted from pages 502–3.

The advantages to farmers of cooperative membership are several: as individuals farmers have little influence in the market place, but through an organization they can meet power with power; the larger volume handled by the cooperative enables it to employ good managerial skills and get sufficient working capital for research and development. It is claimed that the family farm in the United States could not long survive as an atomist unit in our society without the aid of cooperative organizations; they give farmers a sense of belonging and increase their business capabilities through economic information gained in the membership meetings or through published materials. The high-water mark for the number of marketing, farm supply, and related service cooperatives in the United States was 12,000 in 1930. The reduction since then has been due to mergers and consolidations, leading to an increase in size. As the number of cooperatives has declined, membership has risen.

The importance of the cooperatives to rural people is not always appreciated by urban residents who may not be aware that Sunkist oranges, Land O'Lakes butter and cheese, Diamond walnuts, Ocean Spray cranberries, Rockingham meat, and Norbest turkeys—to mention only a few products—are marketed through farmer-owned cooperatives.[10]

From the sociological standpoint, a marketing cooperative or a credit cooperative may be the very first introduction a farmer in Africa or Asia has to what are essentially Western-oriented organizational practices. Instead of reaching a decision by consensus, it may be done by a majority vote, with the minority having to abide by what the majority says. Instead of making up their rules as they go along, the members may be held to a constitution approved by some agency outside their community. Instead of everyone being equal, there are officers with fixed responsibilities which they exercise not always to the liking of the ordinary member. Some farmers learn in course of time that parliamentary procedures may be manipulated to serve individual ends, particularly if the rest of the membership is apathetic or uninformed. Thus, when a farmer joins an organization for the first time he is asked to accept behavior patterns and norms controlling the carrying out of this behavior. He must also become familiar with new statuses such as secretary, treasurer, or president. As a discussion of other kinds of organizations will show, the very fact of membership, especially active membership, is one of the mechanisms articulating the rural sector into the larger society.

10. Martin A. Abrahamsen, "Cooperatives as a Force for Stronger Ties," in *A Place to Live. Yearbook of Agriculture 1963.* Washington, D.C.: U.S. Department of Agriculture, p. 228.

SOCIETAL PROCESSES
AND ECONOMIC DEVELOPMENT

Rural sociologists are keenly aware of the interrelationships between societal processes and economic development. Three, as described by Wilkening, are:

> *Specialization.* Accompanied by a differentiation of social structure [this] leads to the production of more goods and services with less effort. Hence, through specialization and division of labor, the self-sufficient peasant society is transformed into one in which there are many occupations, and whose products and services are exchanged through a barter or money economy.... Specialization leads to change when resources can be obtained from outside the family, and there is specialization in production among farmers as well as between farmers and other occupations.

> *Integration.* ... the acceptance of innovations requires their integration into patterns with respect to time and space, with respect to status and role, and with respect to the symbolic and value systems of the society. Here Durkheim's distinction between 'mechanical' and 'organic' solidarity is relevant. Mechanical solidarity is based upon the homogeneity of the members of the group, while organic solidarity is based upon the division of labor found in industrialized societies. The first type depends upon a common heritage, norms, and activities; while the latter depends upon complementary roles and activities.

> *Adaptation.* ... (borrowed from biology) This adaptation involves mechanisms for the regulation and control of the environment and for the self-regulation of the individual species as the units or subsystems of the larger systems. (Wilkening then shows the new kinds of self-regulating mechanisms that come into existence with the shift from a subsistence to a market economy.)[11]

These processes are at the social-system level and supplement those that make the individual farmer the target of change.

Economic development, according to Max Weber, is made possible through the growth of impersonal bureaucracies that operate on rational rather than subjective personalized grounds. Eric Wolf has described the role that certain "economic mediators" play in familiarizing the rural sector with this rational approach not usually characteristic of a rural society. They may, at first, interpose themselves between the landlords and dependent peasants to collect rent or interest, or hire and remunerate labor on an impersonal basis. These economic mediators may also be buyers or traders.

11. E. A. Wilkening, "Some Perspectives on Change in Rural Societies," *Rural Sociology*, **29** (March 1964), pp. 3–4, 7, 12.

... [they] are bearers of the process of monetization and the agents of social dissolution; at the same time their obedience to the market demands that they maximize returns, regardless of the immediate consequences of their actions. By rendering the process of commodity-formation bureaucratic and impersonal, they remove themselves physically from these consequences; at the same time they lose their ability to respond to social cues from the affected population. Instead, they couple economic callousness with a particular kind of structurally induced stupidity, the kind of stupidity which ascribes to the people themselves responsibility for the evils to which they are subject....[12]

In a highly developed society such as the United States, the fate of the farmer rides with the impersonal market forces. Vidich and Bensman, in their study of Springdale, a rural community in New York State, discuss the farmer's status in this locality. The status was very low, almost declassed, during the agricultural depression between the two World Wars when the farmer became greatly indebted. In fact, in this community of Springdale the farmer's situation was more extreme than the position of farmers in the nation at large because of the marginal agriculture carried on there. But the situation changed, as economic conditions bettered:

Today the farmer is an important and ascendant segment of the rural middle class. From a position of near bankruptcy in 1933 he had risen (at the time of the field work for this study) to a position of heavy capitalization and social prominence. His rise coincided with the rationalization of marketing procedures (the Federal Milk Price Order in the New York Milk Shed), federal agricultural policies, and the rise in the market value of his products since the early 1940's.[13]

This community study makes clear the articulation of these farmers to the decisions and policies of the larger institutional structures outside the community, but it points out that not all farmers accept them. However, "the rate of status ascendancy of the individual farmer is probably directly related to the extent to which he accepts the preferential treatment accorded him in these larger policy decisions."[14] Because he is connected with the great society to such an extent, the farmer's status in comparison to other local groups in Springdale is relatively independent of local community forces. When this connection has occurred, one can say that *social articulation,* based on such processes as specialization, inte-

---

12. Eric R. Wolf, *Peasant Wars of the Twentieth Century.* New York: Harper & Row, 1969, p. 286.

13. Arthur J. Vidich and Joseph Bensman, *Small Town in Mass Society: Class, Power and Religion in a Rural Community.* Princeton, N.J.: Princeton University Press, 1958, p. 96.

14. *Ibid.,* p. 96.

gration, adaptation, rationalization, and bureaucratization, is surely taking place.

Before leaving the topic of the movement toward a modern agriculture, we should remind ourselves that this movement is very uneven. In fact, the inequalities are frequently glossed over in statistics representing gross averages. These statistics fail to indicate that some are benefiting more than others from the agricultural development that is taking place. One writer notes:

> If we play games with institutions concerned with education and research relating to agriculture and do nothing about improving the terms of trade for rural people—the millions and millions of landless laborers and small holders—the situation will continue to worsen. If we work with institutions designed to offer credit to farmers and others attempting to facilitate supply and marketing—and do nothing about national policies which depress the prices of things which farmers sell and boost the prices of things which farmers buy—the situation will continue to worsen. Thus seriousness, with regard to institutional infrastructure, must relate to the institutionalization of economic power and to drastic shift in the locus of political power.[15]

A workshop on Small Farmer Credit[16] pointed out that new ways must be found to meet the needs of the small farmer because existing credit and other development programs have a strong bias against him; the new technologies reach the larger farmers first since they are better educated and have wider social connections. Extension agents gravitate to the medium-size and larger farmers because they share similar backgrounds and training. Private firms manufacturing supplies work with larger farmers because of private motives and more similar backgrounds. As if these were not sufficient handicaps, market systems are usually oriented to serving the commercial producer, reducing ready access to the small farmer. Cooperatives are often controlled by the larger farmers who restrict services to the small farmers. Finally, the research that produces new technologies (irrigation techniques, design of tractors and implements, etc.) is usually oriented toward the needs of the larger farmers.

These are facts to bear in mind as we move to a consideration of tenure patterns in various parts of the world where the scientific farming is only beginning to penetrate and where the extremes among rural people run much more deeply than that between large and small farmers in an economy already being modernized and articulated into the national society.

15. George H. Axinn, "The Problems of Developing Needed Institutional Infrastructure to Sustain Agricultural Development Technology," Paper prepared for presentation at the annual meeting of the Rural Sociological Society, 24 August 1975, San Francisco, California, p. 4.

16. Ronald Tinnermeier and Chris Dowswell, *Small Farmer Credit.* Workshop Report, Agricultural Development Council, Inc. New York, March 1973.

CHAPTER 5
SOCIAL STRATIFICATION, AGRARIAN REFORM, AND SOCIAL ARTICULATION

This chapter attempts to provide a descriptive picture of rural class differences, particularly with reference to landlord-tenant relations. It does not undertake the analytical approach to social class which would be called for if a Marxist interpretation were being used, or indeed if the discussion were to center around Max Weber's three dimensions of society: the economic order, characterized by social class; the social order, represented by status or station; and the political order, represented by the party. Thus, distinctions are made between stratification and a class system, with somewhat different interpretations depending on one's theoretical position: equilibrium or conflict. Kelly has set forth one framework for the analysis of stratification:

> The social system is considered to be composed not of persons, but of the positions and multiposition complexes: groups, organizations, and communities. Persons hold positions within the various group and multigroup systems to which they belong, and perform roles related to (or comprising) those positions. The total structural behavioral system of all the positions which a person holds in society is called a *station*. Stratification, then refers to the relative location, horizontal and vertical, of persons toward each other in terms of the relative ranking of power, wealth, and honor of their respective stations.[1]

In *Social Classes in Agrarian Societies*, Stavenhagen has provided a penetrating picture of rural social classes viewed in the Marxist perspec

---

1. Drenan Kelley, "Changing Stratification in the Rural South." Paper presented at the joint session of the Rural Sociological Society and the American Sociological Association, San Francisco, California, August 29, 1967.

tive. He argues (1) that social classes have to be seen as part of a social structure to which they have specific relationships; (2) that they are tied to the evolution and development of society; (3) that they are determined by the relations of men to the means of production; (4) that a social class exists only in relation to other classes or as a *function* of others; (5) that classes not only constitute structural elements of society, but also specific politico-economic interest groups which, under special economic circumstances, acquire consciousness of themselves and of these interests, and tend to organize for political action with the goal of capturing the power of the state; and (6) that class struggle and conflict are the expression of the internal contradiction of specific socioeconomic systems.[2] Stavenhagen also points out:

> Whereas stratifications represent value systems which claim to have universal validity, class oppositions, on the contrary, create conflicting value systems. As a result, the contradictions that may arise between a stratification system and a class structure imply multiple conflicts between value systems.[3]

What is clear from a study of Marxist analysis is that any systematic treatment of social classes must be carried out for a specific society at definitely stated periods of time, since relations between classes are in dynamic flux. For example, in his conclusions about agrarian reform in the United States, Meadows indicates that the American farmer was from the very beginning an entrepreneur and that his class struggles were intraclass, not counter-class struggles.[4]

Although many factors play a part in any rural stratification system, without question the ownership of and access to the land is the key factor. This leads into the analysis of agrarian structures and the social arrangements governing the control and use of agricultural land.[5] It also leads into a consideration of agrarian reforms occurring in many parts of the world and their effects on stratification and other parts of the social structure.

2. Rodolfo Stavenhagen, *Social Classes in Agrarian Societies,* Garden City, New York: Anchor Press/Doubleday, 1975, pp. 25–32.

3. *Ibid.,* p. 35.

4. Paul Meadows, *The Masks of Change: Essays on Development Roles and Actors,* Syracuse: Center for Overseas Research, Maxwell Graduate School, Syracuse University, December 1964, p. 39.

5. Boguslaw Galeski, *Basic Concepts of Rural Sociology.* Manchester: The University Press. 1972, pp. 110–11. (Translated from the Polish: *Sociologia wsi: pojecia podstawowe.*)

TYPES OF OWNER-TENANT RELATIONS

By using six general types, one can document, in at least rudimentary fashion, the organization of land ownership and the relationship between those who work the land with those who own it, though these may at times be the same.[6]

Tribal Ownership. Tribal leaders assign to members the right to cultivate specific plots of land. Buying, selling, and renting are not involved. In many parts of Africa south of the Sahara, the traditional land tenure system was communal. Individuals and families held and used land ultimately vested in the community. Their "rights in this land existed by virtue of their membership in the relevant social unit. Hence, title to land has a communal character and it is usufructuary, rather than absolute. A chief, for example, may be the custodian of the land but he is not its owner."[7]

Feudal Tenure. Under feudal tenure, which predominated in Europe centuries before the industrial revolution, serfs were attached to property held "in fief" and they were transferable with it. In this system landlords own large areas and command the services of or receive rents from the cultivators and workers who occupy and labor on the estate, plantation, or hacienda. In Latin America this hacienda or latifundia system finds the most fertile and favorably located land in the hands of the members of the few richest and most powerful families, who usually do not live on the estate but leave its management to persons with little training in modern agriculture and animal husbandry. On many of these estates there is a preference for a rudimentary type of cattle ranching and not for growing food and other crops.[8]

Rental Systems. Rental systems, according to the typology used here, are those in which leaseholders or renters produce more than their

6. This typology is adapted from an article by Howard W. Beers, "Socio-Economic Development and Man-Land Relationships," *Sociologia Ruralis*, **8** (1968): 3–4, pp. 331–61.

7. United Nations, Department of Economic Affairs, *Land Reform: Defects in Agrarian Structure as Obstacles to Economic Development*, New York, 1951, p. 28.

8. T. Lynn Smith, "Sociocultural Systems that Obstruct Increased Production of Food in Latin America," prepared for presentation at the annual meeting of the Association for Latin American Studies, New York, November 9, 1968. Mimeographed, p. 15. Also see Roger W. Findley, "Problems Faced by Colombia's Agrarian Reform Institute in Acquiring and Distributing Land," in Robert E. Scott (ed.), *Latin American Modernization Problems: Case Studies in the Crises of Change*. Urbana: University of Illinois Press, 1973, pp. 122–92.

own subsistence requirement, and pay the landlord in kind or cash but are not obliged to render service. This system participates in a money (exchange) economy. Terms of rental are unwritten more often than written, but more and more renting is done by contract which regularizes the arrangement and secures the interest and status of the renter. Thus, the servile status is avoided.

Such security of tenure is lacking in regions of the developing countries of Asia, Latin America, and the Middle East, particularly because of exorbitant rent charges. Where payment of rent is made on a fixed cash basis, the entire burden of risk is passed on to the cultivator. The tenant's security lies in customary agreements, which may or may not be embodied in legislation, but in whose enforcement the tenant has little legal redress.

Such a system has obvious disadvantages to economic development: (1) the tenant has little incentive to increase his output since a large share of any such increase will accrue to the landlord; (2) the peasant is usually left with a bare subsistence minimum and has no margin for investment; and (3) wealth held in the form of land and accumulation of capital does not lead to productive investment. Where the landlord is also the money-lender, as in much of Asia, he depends more upon interest on loans to small cultivators than on increased income from the improvement of land.[9]

But there is another side to the tenancy system which is illustrated by the experience in the United States. Clawson has described it as follows:

> In times past, the presence of a mixed tenure system (both operator-ownership and leasing being important in many areas) has been interpreted as a system of open opportunities for advancement of young farm people. This advancement was often thought of as an "agricultural ladder." A young man might start out as a hired hand, then advance to tenant farmer, later accumulate enough savings to buy a farm of his own, and perhaps finally be sufficiently well off to own some extra land which he leases ("farmer-landlord"), and finally retire to live on his savings and on the rent from his land. Thus there was a "ladder" of four or five "rungs" on which the industrious and the thrifty could advance economically and socially.[10]

Although the ladder concept was unreal to the black croppers of the Southern plantation area, the concept was working usefully in many parts of the country up until World War I. According to Clawson, it contributed to the degree of social mobility and the lack of sharp class distinc-

9. United Nations, *Land Reform*, p. 15.

10. Marion Clawson, *The Land System of the United States: An Introduction to the History and Practice of Land Use and Land Tenure*, Lincoln: University of Nebraska Press, 1968, pp. 100–101.

tions that characterized life in most of the United States, but perhaps most of all in the Midwest.

> ... Social mobility is now largely (although far from perfectly) secured by other economic forces, but the classical ladder concept has become less and less operational as the capital requirements rose. To own a farm through most of his life, a farmer now should have inherited some of its value; to assemble it all through savings from his labor and management earnings is increasingly difficult.[11]

The current trend is toward part-owner, part-tenant farms, since many farmers have inherited farms that are too small to farm alone. Instead of buying more land to get sufficient acreage for efficient farming, they prefer to put their capital into equipment and to lease additional land.

Owner-operators.   Owner-operator is the type generally conceded to provide most production incentive to the cultivator, who receives all returns from management, labor, and investment in land. He makes his own cropping decisions within limits of tradition, technology, market factors, and available resources.

Since the days of Thomas Jefferson, official United States government policy has been to extol and try to strengthen the owner-operated family farm. A United States State Department publication, *Land Reform: A World Challenge*, reaffirms this and describes such a farm as:

> Of the size necessary to maintain a family at a fair living standard and which can be operated by the farmer and his family either alone or with the help of one or two "hired men" who are usually regarded as part of the family group. These farms, of course, vary greatly in size. In the rich valleys of California five acres may be large enough for a lettuce grower; in our Pacific Northwest ten acres may be sufficient for the producer of strawberries. In Iowa's rich cornland 160 acres may be a desirable size. To raise beef cattle on the ranges of our Southwest, 1,000 acres is necessary. ...[12]

Before World War II, trends seemed to favor greater rural stratification and the lessening of the middle-class mentality of the family-sized farm community. Today, hundreds of thousands of farm operators have bought and paid for their farms in full, taking advantage of the fact that earlier mortgage indebtedness could be more easily covered during a period of rapid inflation and rising prices of farm products.

---

11. *Ibid.*, p. 101.

12. United States Department of State, *Land Reform: A World Challenge*, Publication 4445, February 1952, pp. 34–35.

Cooperative Farming. In this system, rights to land and its yield and duties to till it are diffused among members of a local group. Examples of this type are not common enough to make it a major form of land tenure, nor one that persists for a long period without a set of policies enforced by the national government. Spontaneous generation of such cooperation is rare and has little staying power.

One of the features of the Mexican agrarian reform is the development of the *ejido*, in which land belongs to the village but may be farmed individually.

> The *ejido* community, as a landholding unit, was designed by Mexico's land reformers to prevent a return to the excessive concentration of land in large estates, characteristic of pre-revolutionary days, with their negative social, economic, and political implications. About one-half of the agricultural labor force finds employment in the *ejido* sector, which also controls over 40 percent of all crop land in the country. . . .
> . . . In some of these areas, the land reform beneficiaries joined efforts to cultivate their land and apply these inputs cooperatively, thus, in fact, forming what have come to be known as "*collective ejidos.*"
> In their early stages these cooperatives were fairly successful, not only in terms of productivity and income, but also because they contributed to the social solidarity and well-being of previously exploited *peons* and farm laborers. For some years after their establishment, government policy was highly favorable to these experiments.
> However, after a few years things began to change. Public policy turned against the collective *ejidos* and pressures built up through the *ejido* bank and the official peasant organizations to have them transformed into individual *ejidos,* that is, where every farmer cultivates his own plot by himself. . . . Without institutional support at the national level, the cooperative spirit was unable to cope with internal dissention, factionalism, jealousies and vested interests in the community, much of which, in fact, was specifically furthered by forces outside the *ejido* itself.[13]

Israel, too, has experimented with cooperative farms in an effort to settle large numbers of immigrants. The majority of recent settlements are either *moshavim* (where individual families tend their own private holdings, but cooperate), or (to a smaller extent) *kibbutzim* (where all operations are on a collective basis). In the *moshav* each family lives in its own house, cultivates its own holdings, and makes managerial decisions. Seventy to eighty small holdings usually compose a *moshav*. The cooperative has only limited control over the production enterprise. However, it provides all the municipal and economic services for its mem-

13. Rodolfo Stavenhagen, "A Land Reform Should Answer the Questions It Raises: An Analysis of this Century's First Experiment," *Ceres,* **2** (November–December 1969), pp. 43–45. Also see Nathan L. Whetten, *The Role of the Ejido in Mexican Land Reform.* University of Wisconsin Land Tenure Center, Paper 3, May 1963.

bers, for which taxes are levied on the farmers. Similarly all agricultural requisites (water, fertilizer, seed, feed stuffs, etc.) are provided through the cooperative on credit recoverable from incoming returns. The *kibbutz* is said to have certain advantages in that it can specialize in a limited number of branches on a relatively large scale of operation. It can make optimal advantage of its location (water, climate, etc.) and make the most effective use of farm mechanization.

The Communist regimes of Eastern Europe carried out the most extensive effort yet undertaken to create "cooperative farms." (See the case of Komárov, p. 21.) There were several forms of these, depending upon what the cooperator contributed to the overall enterprise: land, animals, or labor. The eventual goal, however, was to form the peasants, many of whom had previously been independent owners, into a collective farm (the *kolkhoz*) reminiscent of the type that Stalin had developed in the Soviet Union.

These various types—*ejido, kibbutz, moshav, kolkhoz*—though differing considerably from each other represent efforts at cooperative farming based on some aspect of collective ownership.

Large Scale Business and State Farms. In capitalist societies, there is an increasing tendency to apply business practices to agriculture to the point that we now speak of "agro-business" and insist that a would-be farmer in agricultural college receive training in business techniques and decision-making. Such a farm may be made up of land that the operator or corporation owns plus much that is leased or rented, but the key to success lies in management techniques and the mixing of the factors of production into profit-making proportions. This moves beyond the simpler family-type farm of the early American settlers or of the European peasant proprietor of today. It maximizes economy of scale and occasionally makes use of seasonal wage labor. It does not have the tenancy feature of the older plantation or of the Latin American *latifundia*, but it does rely on size of holding as a major feature.

Somewhat comparable to this large-scale privately run commercial farm is the similarly large-scale state farm, found principally in the Communist areas of Eastern Europe. At the time of the postwar land reforms in these countries, a proportion of the expropriated land was formed into state-operated farms, similar to the *sovkhozi* in the Soviet Union. These have been likened to "grain factories," and they were thought of as the mechanism whereby industrial techniques would be applied to agriculture. They, too, use wage labor and invest heavily in equipment.

In view of these varying tenure and related stratification patterns, it should not be surprising that there are also several approaches to land reform.

TYPES OF AGRARIAN REFORM

Land reform programs have been classified into four types on the basis of the extent to which they exercise public controls over individual action:[14]

Mild Reforms. These include (1) laws governing landlord-tenant relations and leasing arrangements; (2) land settlement and development programs; (3) measures for the provision of agricultural credit facilities; and (4) authority for voluntary land consolidation commissions.

Public Controls Short of Expropriation. Most important examples of this type are those dealing with rent control or rent reduction and those dealing with mandatory land consolidation. Also important are measures to prevent the parceling of land and to limit the extent of land ownership.

> In Pakistan land reform was not part of a productivity drive nor was it a matter of doing away with sharecropping or rendering supporting services. It was simply a program of fixing ceilings to the size of individual owner- ship, and taking away some of the land from the largest owners.[15]

Land Expropriation Programs. Some landowners are divested of all or part of their holdings, usually by public action. In most cases they have been compensated. The land thus obtained is usually placed in a national land pool for state uses or for direct redistribution to tenants, landless workers, and small peasant proprietors. The new owner is ex- pected to make some payment for his land, ranging from an amount equal to one or two times the annual value of the crop to the current market value of the land. The government helps the new owner obtain long-term credit with repayment arrangements made so as to accommo- date the new owners.[16]

A survey of such programs reveals that in most cases only modest amounts of land become available for distribution since those holding large tracts destined for expropriation can shift some land to exempted uses (such as orchards), and can deed acreages of the size permitted under the law to relatives. Then, too, since most legislatures in countries experi- encing such land reforms are heavily influenced by large landowners,

---

14. Raleigh Barlowe, "Land Reform and Economic Development," *Journal of Farm Economics*, **35** (May 1953).

15. Arthur Gaitskell, "A Mid-Course Solution," *Ceres*, **2** (Dec. 1969), pp. 34–35.

16. Barlowe, *Land Reform*, pp. 5–6.

legal means are frequently used to postpone or forestall the benefits that would be passed on to the new owners. Or, to put it bluntly, the government officials charged with carrying out the reforms do it half-heartedly. The cases of thorough-going expropriation and redistribution occur in a revolutionary period such as the French Revolution, the Russian Revolution, the Mexican Revolution, and the changes in East European countries in the wake of World War II.

Collectivization Programs.   As has already been mentioned, in the Soviet Union, and in other East European countries, peasant proprietors were persuaded to join the cooperative or collective farms. In these countries, much official stress is placed on the voluntary character of these "cooperative farms," but most of those joining had little other choice when they joined because of the political and social pressures brought to bear. When the collectivization drive was halted in Yugoslavia and Poland, most peasants opted for the family farm. Today, however, where collective farmers have become habituated to the cooperative pattern, many would choose the collective to the responsibilities of operating a family farm.

The economic and social effects of these reforms will certainly vary with the type and the thoroughness of the reforms and the political purposes the reforms were to serve. They will differ in the extent to which they will lead toward social articulation.

AGRARIAN REFORM AND SOCIAL ARTICULATION

A conclusion reached by all students of agrarian reform is that the mere act of land redistribution must be accompanied by a number of other services (credit, transportation, advisory services, etc.) if it is to have long-term, positive economic effects. In fact, some contend that "rural development that accents capital investment and technological improvements is far more likely to produce a significant rise in rural living standards than is land redistribution."[17] This is another way of saying that the new owner must be included in the economic networks necessary for improved agriculture, those in which the landlord or his agents participated previously.

Often the political goals of agrarian reform are as important to the

17.   Charles J. Erasmus, "Agrarian vs. Land Reform: Three Latin-American Countries," in Philip K. Bock (Ed.), *Peasants in the Modern World*, Albuquerque: University of New Mexico Press, 1969, p. 23.

government leaders as the economic goals. They hope to link the rural society more fully to the national society. In some cases, this is to dispel unrest and to placate members of rural society by a land redistribution scheme. Or it may be, as in the case of some East European countries, to change the agrarian structure so as to eliminate a land-owning peasantry as a social class and convert rural people into collective farmers more in tune with socialist objectives. Some regimes carry out land reform in the name of "democratization" in the hope of creating a new social structure characterized by increased political participation of the rural people and not necessarily as members of a rural proletariat.

In his study of three Latin American agrarian reforms Erasmus points out that in Bolivia the land-tenure reform was an integral part of a revolution. The peasants were organized into peasant syndicates which initiated the expropriation of hacienda land and simultaneously became the means of consolidating the rural masses behind the revolutionary party. "Once the formation of peasant syndicates had been justified and implemented through land reform, the party in power could use them at election time to amass the show of votes with which it legitimized its authority."[18] Erasmus concludes, however, that it takes a broader agrarian-reform program than land redistribution to maintain peasant unions as vote-buying mechanisms. He, too, stresses the point that there must also be programs of farm credit, housing, road building, machinery, etc., for these provide local peasant leaders with many goals for rural improvements to which they can redirect their political activities after their request for land has been met. "In short, true redistribution of political influence in the rural sector tends to be associated with the economic and technological developments that progressively lift standards and aspirations—not with land redistribution per se."[19] One of the most obvious effects of agrarian reform is the stratification patterns of rural areas. In Japan, for instance, under the reform laws:

> ... all the land of absentee landlords and all leased-out land of village landlords in excess of one hectare was purchased by the State and resold to tenants. The practice, until then general, of paying rents in kind was forbidden, and cash payment was required. Moreover, rents were controlled; landlords could no longer demand rents at a level which had justly been described as feudal. This reform was practically completed within the short space of a little over two years and as a result the area of tenanted land, which before the war had been approximately 53 percent for rice land and 40 percent for dry land, fell to below 10 percent.[20]

18. *Ibid.*, p. 25.

19. *Ibid.*, pp. 26–27.

20. Tadashi Fukutake, *Japanese Rural Society*, Oxford: Oxford University Press, 1967, p. 18.

Since the reform, stratification by ownership status has ceased to mean very much, according to Professor Fukutake. In this sense, there has been much equalization. Wolf Ladejinsky notes that agrarian reform can narrow the traditional differences in the class structure of the village. "As the tenants step up, the landlords step down. As the landlord loses much of his affluence, he loses much of his influence. This does not presuppose that the resident landlord is completely displaced or that it is necessary to eliminate him altogether. What is taking place now in the Japanese village is the sharing of power between the old and new leadership."[21]

The situation was quite different in Taiwan. Gallin points out that traditionally the village landlord has played the major leadership role in his village and surrounding area and that this role was further buttressed during the period of Japanese occupation. These authorities preferred to work through the landlords rather than deal directly with the peasants; also, the peasants realized that if they were to get along with the Japanese, they would have to work through the landlords. So they elected the landlord to handle local affairs and to represent village interests.

This arrangement was to the landlord's advantage. As the official village leader, he wielded greater power by which he could more easily manipulate the villagers, and even the tax collector and others to his own advantage. Recognition as a leader by his fellow villagers and by the authorities also increased his prestige in the area. Not only was such a landlord the elected village political leader but he often was an informal leader as well—a person who assumed an active part in most of the social and religious affairs of the village. He usually contributed time and money to help make these affairs a success. Such efforts by the landlord helped to build his reputation as a public-spirited person.

Frequently, the landlord assumed the role of mediator in discussions of village or inter-village problems and in disputes between his own villagers or between members of other villages. . . .

These conditions continued after the Restoration into the post-Land Reform period. Today, the landlord class continues in the rural areas and wields power in local grass-root politics as well as in socioeconomic affairs. In many villages, the recognized leaders are still those who are rich, maintain big landholdings, and have had a fairly good education. Such people are also known to have influence in some government agency. It is still an advantage for a village to have a wealthy representative of the landlord class to deal with the authorities since most of the local government officials are also drawn from the same class.[22]

21. Wolf I. Ladejinsky, "Land Reform," in Seven Articles on Land Reform, Michigan State University Asian Studies Papers, Reprint Series No. 2, 1964–65, p. 76.

22. Bernard Gallin, "Social Effects of Land Reform in Taiwan." Reproduced by permission of the Society for Applied Anthropology from Human Organization, 22 (Summer, 1963): 2, pp. 109–12.

Gallin also notes that matters are changing as many formerly large landholders and traditional village leaders are giving up their major economic interests in the land. When this occurs, they also lose interest in the village and give less time and money to its affairs. It is no longer to their personal advantage to maintain a leadership role. They may even shift their residence from the village to a place nearer their new economic interests. Thus, village and intervillage problems go unresolved. Some villages react to this loss of leadership with apathy—a reluctance to occupy positions of formal village leadership. Others try to get people not of the landlord class to run for mayor, but with mixed success. This does indicate, however, "the beginning of a crack in the traditional social system which had grown out of the unequal distribution of rural wealth and income as a result of the land-tenure system."[23]

The illustrations cited in previous sections show that historically the landlords have provided the bridge between their tenants and workers and the larger society. They were the connecting link with the national economy, the political system, and with "the people of the world," as peasants sometimes refer to those outside the rural sector. Some landlords were absentee, preferring to dwell in the city and share in its amenities. They left the management of their estates up to others. Some landlords were entrepreneurs, however, and devoted their own time and attention to improving farming practices and thereby increasing their income. They "administered justice" on their estates and provided the material and welfare needs they thought necessary to their tenants.

Therefore, one effect of full-scale land reform is the elimination or lessening of the influence of the landlords, thus breaking the connecting link that they provided. The responsibilities for interacting with the various economic, political, and educational functionaries either devolves upon the new individual owner or upon some new semigovernmental device set up as a substitute for the landlord or his agents. In some cases, the owner-operators are able to assume these responsibilities because of their former activities as tenants and their social contacts outside their own village; elsewhere, production falls drastically when outside management is provided as part of the land reform program.

Many approaches are used to help create ties between the new owners and the more modern sector of the society. In the United States in the days of the New Deal, the Farm Security Administration (FSA) was set up to help tenant farmers, particularly in the South, acquire land of their own. One provision insisted upon by the FSA was that both the new owner and his wife work with agricultural and home demonstration

23. *Ibid.*, p. 112.

agents, who would help the couple draw up a plan for operating the farm and household and for financing the obligations they had assumed. In Mexico, the *ejido* was another kind of substitute for the landlord. In Egypt, recipients of land whose holdings totaled less than six acres (five feddans) were required to belong to cooperative societies designed to aid in production, marketing, and credit under government supervision and guidance.

On the surface, this might seem to be trading one kind of paternalism (governmental) for another (landlord), but the social meaning is much deeper than this. As a result of the reform, *external agents* become the intermediaries between the rural people and the outside world. No one person, such as the landlord, embodies the whole series of connections; rather, representatives of several governmental agencies become available.

And, finally, what are the psychological effects of their new status on rural people? Experience shows that the first flush of enthusiasm for the government which provided them with the land (for which they are expected to pay something at least), can turn to disappointment and resentment if they are not afforded ways of forming satisfactory connections with the groups outside their village or farmsteads upon whom they are dependent for even a modest approach toward scientific farming. Thus agrarian reform, as its most astute observers continue to point out, is much more than land redistribution; it also involves the participation of the beneficiaries of the reform in a wide variety of connections which directly tie them more fully to the nonrural aspects of their society. This is why it is no longer possible to think in terms of only the rural-class system, for the interaction between the self-conscious rural dwellers and the various urban classes becomes significant in any program of national development. Class groups interpenetrate and a rural set of criteria for determining social stratification inevitably will reflect more strongly the criteria used in the urban areas. In fact, this is one condition for pervasive social articulation.

One common aspect of the landlord-tenant relationship in some countries was the symbolic identification made by the tenants with the family owning the estate. In a very real psychological sense, the villagers "belonged" to the family. But through various legislative acts in the last two or three generations, the bonds have become much looser. As the landlords disappear, what takes their place? The obvious answer is the national leader does, partciularly if he has a charismatic quality. He is the one who has "given the peasant his land;" he stands for the dawning of a new day. Nationalism tends more and more to replace localism; rural people are caught up in something outside their own village. Of course, agrarian reform is not totally responsible for nor a necessary condition for this transfer of allegiance to the national state. Yet it does represent one of the major steps which a developing country can take.

From the sociological standpoint, therefore, the test of agrarian reform lies in the extent to which the new owners can function successfully in their new status in their local agricultural network. How are they helped to move from the status of tenants or landless workers to owners, with all that this involves in decision-making on many fronts? What links do they establish, in lieu of the landlord, with persons and agencies that provide supplies (seeds, fertilizers, farm equipment, etc.), that buy their crops, or that advise them on better ways of farming? And what is their experience with the national legal system that provides them with patents of ownership or gives them security in leasing arrangements if they are still part-tenants?

CHAPTER 6
THE RURAL FAMILY, FAMILISM, AND DEMOGRAPHIC CHANGE

The population explosion, which has become a world-wide concern, is closely linked to the rural family. The possibility of the world's people outstripping the food supply depends in part upon (1) whether the rural families curtail the number of births and (2) whether they will adopt more efficient farming practices to meet increased food requirements. Because it combines within a single institution both the biological and economic functions, the family in rural society appears vividly in a central position in that society. On a family farm there is a common preoccupation with the agricultural enterprise, supported in many countries by the folk belief that security lies in a large number of children who can help with the farm work and also take care of the parents in their old age.

CENTRALITY OF THE FAMILY IN RURAL SOCIETIES

The centrality of the family can be demonstrated by (1) indicating the significant functions it performs and (2) showing the nature of *familism* and its pervasiveness in rural societies.

Functions

The functions that the family as an institution performs for the members of a society can be grouped under four main headings: biological, psychological, sociological, and economic.

Biological. As societies modernize, the reproductive function remains important even though the desired size of a family becomes smaller.

Another biological function of the family is that of sustenance, or providing for the physical needs of its members. Rural poverty as well as urban poverty is associated with the inability of the family to meet such needs as food, clothing, and shelter.

Psychological. Socialization is an additional function expected of the family. The role of the elders is to guide the children, as their personalities develop through reacting to the social environment. Children learn the values cherished by those about them, the roles they are expected to play in a given situation, and the penalties or sanctions for failure to conform. In turn, parenthood also socializes adults in new directions. In rural societies, the family bears a heavier responsibility for socialization, which in urban societies may be shared more deliberately with the school, religious, and "character-building" groups, or unintentionally with peer groups whose members may oppose parental admonitions.

A sense of security, which seems to be a universal human urge, has also been traditionally found in the family group. Many students of the family contend that a joint, *extended family*, where, for example, two or three married brothers and their families live in the same compound, affords a greater sense of psychological security than the small, *nuclear family* consisting only of husband, wife, and offspring. In the extended family, the argument goes, there are other adults to substitute for a parent who is ill, away at work, or deceased. In some joint families, however, there is so much bickering and conflict that some members (often wives, who come from the outside) would prefer to live separately with their immediate family, and not in the larger group. Some observe that the privacy of the smaller nuclear family, despite its fragility, may give to those involved greater psychological security in the sense of personal fulfillment and deeper creativity than the extended family. Yet, whatever its size or structure, one function of the family is to meet affectional needs as well as to afford a sense of physical and psychological security.

Sociological. A family obviously gives each individual his start in life. This is a "headstart" if one comes from a family unit above average in income and social standing. Thus one function of the rural family is to help individuals "locate" themselves in a rural society where other people tend to rank them in terms of family background. In a caste society, the rank is often considered God-given and individuals can do little to change their position, but in most societies there are paths which individuals can follow if they seek a position higher than that of their parents. If they stay in the rural community, acquisition of more land might lead to an improved status or marriage into one of the highly regarded well-established families. Otherwise, they can migrate to a town or city.

At times the family is expected to exercise direct social control over members who may be departing from accepted practices. Parents rather than social workers or juvenile-court officials bring erring young people into line. In return for conformity to social norms, young people also have the right to expect that their elders will protect and stand by them when necessary.

The rural family also plays an important sociological function in helping satisfy the recreational needs of its members. Kinship underlies the celebration of feast days, visiting with relatives who live in another community, and even the introduction of young people into adult recreation (young women into women's recreational groups; young men into tavern groups).

Economic. As mentioned in earlier chapters, the division of labor within the family is supervised by the family head. Therefore, a family works together in order to meet its major economic needs. At times, if the farm is too small to provide adequate support, some family members may seek work elsewhere and send money back home. In a traditional society, the claims of one's relatives upon earnings and economic resources are very great, at times causing the individual to sacrifice his own economic interests in order to serve the larger family group.

This is seen in another economic function—namely, the care of the elderly. National planners, who are usually urban-oriented, often fail to recognize the great contributions that rural families make to the national economy by the very fact that they offer a haven for those too old to support themselves. If the state had to provide homes, emotional support, and even food for these senior citizens in rural areas, it would face staggering costs. The same applies to other incapacitated members, whether physically handicapped or mentally ill, who live in a rural family circle.

In addition to the above, the family in most societies is the mechanism for passing on economic possessions from one generation to the next.

These biological, psychological, sociological, and economic functions combine in familism a distinctive way of organizing a society.

Familism

In a pioneering work in rural sociology, Kulp highlights the centrality of the family in a village in traditional South China:

Familist arrangements and practices are the core of the village community. All purposes, all proposals, all conduct, all gains, all standards and ideals are referred to and evaluated by comparison with the fortunes of familist groupings, economic, religious and sib. Whatever conduces to the welfare of the members of these familist groups, to the performance of their special functions, maintenance or worship, is good; everything else is bad.[1]

Kulp then defines familism as "a form of social organization in which all values are determined by reference to the maintenance, continuity and functions of family groups."[2]

Key elements of familism are shown on a familism scale.[3] Table 6-1 shows the scores for four different groups: Column A—young rural Greeks; B—Mennonite college students in the Midwest; C—Methodist college students in Michigan; D—Michigan urban high-school students who were Methodists. A score of four would mean that everyone in the group agreed with the statement; one or zero would mean that none agreed.

Bardis draws three conclusions from the scores of these four groups: first, the Greeks were more familistic than the other three groups; second, the religion of the Mennonites seems quite influential since their scores were higher than those of the Methodists though lower than those of the Greeks; and third, age appears to have a significant effect on familism scores as shown by the fact that the younger Methodist high-school students had higher familistic scores than the older Methodist college students. These findings become clearer, however, if one compares the more urban-oriented college students (Column C) with the Greek peasant youths (Column A) on specific items such as 3, 6, 8, 13.

Sorokin has developed the idea of familistic-contractual relations.[4] Familistic relations are closely associated with the kinship group where people are valued for their own sake; the individual is willing to sacrifice for members of his family, to subordinate himself for the larger good of

1. Daniel Harrison Kulp, II, *Country Life in South China: The Sociology of Familism. Volume I. Phenix Village, Kwantung, China*, New York: Teachers College, Columbia University Press, 1925, p. 187.

2. *Ibid.*, p. 188. The present author's description of familism in Bulgaria in the 1930's parallels in significant ways the findings for the Chinese village. (See *Balkan Village*, Lexington, Ky.: University of Kentucky Press, 1949, pp. 144–147. Also see W. Goldschmidt and E. J. Kunkel, "The Structure of the Peasant Family," *American Anthropologist*, **73** (1971); 1058–1076.

3. Panos D. Bardis, "A Comparative Study of Familism," *Rural Sociology*, **24** (December 1959); 362–371.

4. Pitirim A. Sorokin, Carle C. Zimmerman, and Charles J. Galpin, *A Systematic Source Book in Rural Sociology*, Minneapolis: The University of Minnesota Press, 1931. Vol. II, Chap. X; also, Pitirim A. Sorokin, *The Crisis of Our Age: The Social and Cultural Outlook*. New York: E. P. Dutton, 1941. Chap. V; also *Society, Culture and Personality*. New York: Harper & Row, 1947, pp. 93–118.

Table 6–1   Familism scores of Greeks, Mennonites, and Methodists

SCALE ITEM	A*	B*	C*	D*
1. A person should always support his uncles or aunts if they are in need	2.32	1.87	1.32	1.82
2. Children below 18 should give almost all their earnings to their parents	2.34	1.34	.82	.82
3. The family should consult close relatives (uncles, aunts, first cousins) concerning its important decisions	2.42	1.58	.79	1.84
4. Children below 18 should almost always obey their older brothers and sisters	3.05	1.66	1.42	1.68
5. A person should always consider the needs of his family as a whole more important than his own	3.21	2.63	2.26	3.13
6. At least one married child should be expected to live in the parental home	2.76	.71	.16	.37
7. A person should always be expected to defend his family against outsiders even at the expense of his own personal safety	3.71	2.18	2.53	3.21
8. The family should have the right to control the behavior of each of its members completely .	3.26	1.21	.82	1.21
9. A person should always support his parents-in-law if they are in need	2.26	2.45	2.16	2.11
10. A person should always avoid every action of which his family disapproves	3.32	1.11	1.37	1.79
11. A person should always share his home with his uncles, aunts, or first cousins if they are in need	2.26	1.55	1.13	1.84
12. A person should always be completely loyal to his family	3.58	2.24	2.16	3.05
13. The members of a family should be expected to hold the same political, ethical, and religious beliefs	2.37	1.34	.68	.50
14. Children below 18 should always obey their parents	3.68	2.32	2.29	2.74
15. A person should always help his parents with the support of his younger brothers and sisters if necessary	3.79	2.74	2.61	3.16
16. A person should always share his home with his parents-in-law if they are in need . . .	2.42	2.11	1.89	2.05
Total	46.75	29.04	24.41	31.32

*A, Greeks; B, Mennonites; C, Methodist college students; D, Methodist high-school students.
Source: Panos A. Bardis, "A Comparative Study of Familism," Rural Sociology, 24 (December 1959), pp. 364–365.

the family. The "we" identification is very important. In contrast, in a contractual relationship, other people become instrumental to the end one has in view. One gains at the expense of the other: the merchant—buyer; the employer—employee; the banker—borrower. Sorokin shows, however, that these considerations permeate many noneconomic relationships in the contractual-type society. It might be added that members of a major profession—lawyers—devote much of their time to the interpretation of these contractual relationships. This means that in contractual relations one does not accept a person's word as a guarantee as one does in a familistic society. Increasingly one insists that any kind of agreement be in writing. Rights of family members become codified in law: inheritance, marriage and divorce arrangements, and regulations controlling child labor and working hours for women. One measure of articulation, then, is the degree to which contractual relations have replaced familistic ones.

DEMOGRAPHIC TRENDS: A FAMILY MATTER

Rural-urban differences show up not only in family types and in the quality of social relationships but in demographic patterns as well. These can be seen in a discussion of population numbers and of the migration of rural people.

Population Numbers

Reference has already been made to the debate about the possibility of population numbers outstripping the food supply. By the year 2000 the global population may be 6.5 billions (some say 8 billions) as compared with the 1970 figure of 3.6 billions.

In 1950, 71.8 percent of the world's population was thought to be rural, but in 1970 it was estimated at 61 percent, or a decrease of 14.4 percent in twenty years.[5] In contrast the United States was 61 percent rural in 1910, as compared with 26.5 percent in 1970. The term *rural* in the United States includes anyone living in settlements of less than 2,500, thus including many people not in agriculture. People living on *farms* comprise less than five percent of the population of the United States.

5. Kingsley Davis, "The Role of Urbanization in the Development Process," *International Technical Cooperation Centre Review* (Tel Aviv), 1 (July 1972), p. 2.

Family size tends to be larger among rural people than urban people. This holds true if one counts all of the people residing in the household or only the nuclear family. The household of three members is a distinctive feature of modern industrialized nations; five or more members characterize the family units in the less urbanized developing countries.

It is generally assumed that death rates are lower in rural than in urban areas, though some question the official statistics used in arriving at this conclusion. One study found that in India and Taiwan there was higher mortality in rural than in urban areas. This poses the question of whether this might be true for other countries if only more accurate indices were available.[6]

Another feature of rural people is their high birth rates. As a rule, rural fertility rates in almost all countries and in every state of the United States are higher than urban fertility rates. The farm people truly constitute the seedbed of most nations.

The 1970 United States Census shows that farm women bear about 20 percent more children than women in nonfarm areas, but an analysis of fertility in the state of Kentucky shows, however, that the rural and urban differences are becoming less. The reason lies not so much in the reduction of rural fertility but in the more marked increase in fertility in urban areas.[7]

Another important rural-urban difference is found in the composition of the population. Usually, there are more males than females on farms. In the United States in 1969 the figure was 106 males for every 100 females, while for the nonfarm, civilian, noninstitutional population the figure was 92 males to 100 females. Reasons for this discrepancy are that women make the short-distance migrations from the farms, immigrants (chiefly male) move to farms as well as cities, and more older people are women. In some rapidly industrializing countries, the males migrate to the cities in such numbers that authorities worry about "the feminization of the countryside."

As compared with the urban population, the rural-farm population consists of large proportions of young (under 20) and a larger share of those between 45 and 64. Thus, the load of dependency is much higher for farm than for urban populations.

This greatly abbreviated review of some of the facts concerned with population numbers shows the continuing importance of the biological

6. Eduardo E. Arriaga, "Rural-Urban Mortality in Developing Countries: An Index for Detecting Rural Underregistration," *Demography*, **4** (December 1967), pp. 98–107.

7. Eun Sul Lee, "Trends in Fertility Differentials in Kentucky," *Rural Sociology*, **37** (September 1972), pp. 389–400.

function of rural families even though differences between rural and urban demographic characteristics lessen with increasing modernization.

Migration

Migration constitutes the major process whereby the rural and urban sectors become articulated in the demographic sense.

Three interesting aspects of migration are (1) its absorption of surplus labor; (2) the characteristics of those who migrate; and (3) why people move.

Surplus Labor.   Because of decreased mortality, the farmer has more children surviving to early adulthood than did his parents who may have experienced a similar number of live births. The children become surplus in two senses: their total labor is not needed and the land, if divided among all of the children, is too small in area to support them all. Consequently, some must move off the land. In earlier days in the United States and in some countries experiencing new settlement programs today, those leaving a particular farm could remain in the rural areas and open up new farm land of their own. A few might migrate abroad or to a major city, but farming remained the chief attraction where land was available.

Because of the closing of the frontier and an increasing demand for available arable land, the town and city proved the major population outlet. Labor was needed in building roads, railroads, construction, mining, and other extractive enterprises. As industry developed, it required increasing numbers of both male and female workers. And at a later stage, urban service industries—dry cleaning, restaurants, recreation centers, government jobs—all needed more employees than the city was able to provide out of its own natural increase. So migrants made up the difference.

Characteristics of Migrants.   Rural sociologists distinguish four types of rural migration within the United States: the first has already been discussed above—from rural to urban areas. A second type is the migration across state lines from a rural area either to another rural area or to the city. A third type is movement from one farm to another in the same state. A fourth is the migratory agricultural labor which follows the crop seasons.[8]

Most studies indicate that rural migrants in the United States come from areas of low economic opportunity, that they are relatively young (in their twenties), and that they number more females than males. On

8.   T. Lynn Smith, *The Sociology of Rural Life*, New York: Harper & Row, 1947, p. 173.

the other hand, there is a tendency for many people over 65 years of age to return from the city to the rural areas where they originated. In the Southern states, the nonwhite migration exceeds the white migration, with nonwhites often going to the North in search of better opportunity.[9]

Families that are well established, even in times of economic stress, prefer to make what is called *stepwise occupational adjustments.* They find, whenever possible, nonfarm employment that permits them to remain in the family home and thereby keep the option of returning to farming if this becomes necessary. The young people, however, tend to migrate outside the area.[10]

Why Rural People Move. There are many theories which undertake to explain why people leave the farm. For example, one study of high-school graduates from counties in two sections of Minnesota stresses the "success theme" as an important explanation of migration:

> By way of theoretical orientation the authors propose that a socio-economic success theme pervades U.S. society and that rural youths accept this theme into their own values. Consequently, each youth seeks communities during his early adult years which he thinks offer him the best opportunity for such success. Some see this opportunity in their hometown; others see brighter opportunities elsewhere.[11]

A study of the counties of Georgia seeks to explain the net migration of males from farms between 1950 and 1960 in terms of economic measures. The decline in crop acreage of the four major farm crops (cotton, corn, peanuts, and tobacco) accounted for slightly over half of the net migration of these males. Other economic indices accounted for up to 77 percent of the migration.[12] Such research reinforces the fact that people move when economic opportunity diminishes.

In the Upper St. John Valley in Maine, a combination of economic and social factors play a part:

9.   Roger L. Burford, *Louisiana's Human Resources: Part IV. Migration of Working Aged Population,* Bulletin No. 595 (May 1965), Department of Rural Sociology, Louisiana State University. Also see C. Horace Hamilton, "Educational Selectivity of Migration from Farm to Urban and to Other Nonfarm Communities," in Mildred B. Kantor (ed.), *Mobility and Mental Health,* New York: Charles C Thomas, 1965. Chap. 7.

10. William W. Reeder and Nelson L. Le Ray, *Farm Families Under Stress: Reactions to Social Change in St. Lawrence County, New York. 1949–1962,* Bulletin 1027 (June 1970), Cornell University Agricultural Experiment Station.

11. Marvin J. Taves and Richard W. Coller, *In Search of Opportunity: A Study of Post High School Migration in Minnesota,* University of Minnesota Agricultural Experiment Station Technical Bulletin 247, 1964, pp. 3–4.

12. Prakash C. Sharma, "Migration From Georgia Farms." Paper prepared for presentation at the Annual Meetings of the Rural Sociological Society, Denver, Colorado, August 1971.

Despite the fact that the wages received by pulp cutters and other woods workers are relatively high for the area, the physical hardships associated with this type of work—severe weather, insects, safety hazards—tend to outweigh the remunerative aspects. Perhaps even more important, although it is difficult to document, is the apparent attitude of many young people that working in the woods is socially unrewarding. Thus, although opportunities for woods related employment exist, young males tend to migrate, particularly to southern New England for industrial employment.[13]

In the same area, changes in potato farming have also contributed to the high rate of outmigration. The small farmer finds it hard to compete with larger mechanized operations.

An explanation for migration has been found in community structure. On the assumption that rural Brazilians migrated only after visiting the city, two investigators studied the contacts that 1,154 farm operators had with cities classified as small (less than 40,000 people), medium (40,000–100,000), and large (over 100,000 cities.[14] A few of the findings are:

1. Medium-sized cities were most frequently visited by the farm operators in the sample considered as a group. But the poorest (subsistence stratum) tended to visit the small cities and the upper strata (latifundista and commercial strata) visited the large cities most often.

2. The highest stratum (latifundista) visited cities more frequently than did other strata.

3. More of the people from closed communities (where land ownership is highly concentrated) visited the cities than did those from open communities. There seemed to be more of a "push" for those in the communities of less opportunity (the closed) and so the poorer people there built up contacts outside, but chiefly in the small or medium city.

This theory assumes that the act of migrating is part of a social network involving previous experiences with the area of destination.

These various approaches to the question of why rural people move illustrate the complexity of the situations. But such factors must be analyzed and evaluated if one is to try to predict migration patterns, a topic of vital interest to those responsible for providing services for those who come to the city.

13. Louis A. Ploch and Nelson L. Le Ray. *Social and Economic Consequences of the Dickey-Lincoln School Hydro-electric Power Development on the Upper St. John Valley, Maine—Phase I, Preconstruction*, Maine Agricultural Experiment Station, Miscellaneous Report 123, March 1968, p. 3.

14. J. David Stanfield and Gordon C. Whiting, "Community Structure and Potential for Migration." Unpublished paper, March 1971. Also see William A. Douglass, "Rural Exodus in Two Spanish Basque Villages: A Cultural Explanation," *American Anthropologist*, **73** (1971); 1100–1114, which stresses community differences in inheritance norms as possible explanation for migration.

CHAPTER 7
THE CHANGING FAMILY AND ARTICULATING NETWORKS

Numerous studies of kinship networks are now appearing as social scientists seek to understand how relationships within the larger family unit change.[1] Some of these changes facilitate articulation with the urban world. In addition, there are new connections between the family units and other parts of the society as the family surrenders some functions to specialized mechanisms (education, recreation, and welfare) developed to meet the needs of a complex society. Some indications of these changes within the family and with external units can be demonstrated.

Demographic Effects

As the size and composition of the family changes, one would expect some modifications in its connections with various social networks.[2] For instance, the presence of an elderly person in the home would involve the family with visitors who come to see this person, with agencies which render service to the elderly, and with other mem-

---

1. John Mogey, "Content of Relations with Relatives," Paper prepared for XIII International Seminar on Family Research, Paris, September, 1973. Contains a good bibliography covering studies of families as social networks. Also see Bert Adams, "Isolation, Function and Beyond: American Kinship in the 1960's," *Journal of Marriage and the Family* (November 1970).

2. Kingsley Davis, "The American Family in Relation to Demographic Change," in Charles F. Westoff and Robert Parke, Jr. (eds.), Commission on Population Growth and the American Future, *Research Reports, Volume I, Demographic and Social Aspects of Population Growth*, pp. 237–65.

bers of the family (brothers and sisters who may live at a distance). When such a person dies and the family becomes a two-generation rather than a three-generation household, social contacts begin to change.

As divorce becomes more common, people may marry at an earlier age, secure in the knowledge that they are not necessarily obliged to stay together the rest of their lives. This, in turn, may raise the number of children born to these couples married at an earlier age.[3]

Furthermore, the interaction within a one-child family, which is often identified with urban apartment living, is different from that within a family with five children, which is not uncommon in rural areas. When the five children grow up and settle down with families of their own, they form an important kinship network that may or may not be cultivated, but that is totally lacking in the one-child family.

Efforts by government or privately sponsored groups to control the birth rate lead to contacts that initially are very strange to rural people.[4] For example, the family planning programs send out teams to rural communities or to selected areas of cities to meet with the women (sometimes with husbands as well) to promote the use of contraception. As Table 7–1 shows, the linkage of a rural family, particularly in nonindustrialized countries, with a family planning program involves more than a simple conversation between a medical professional and a peasant woman. The establishment of such a relationship calls for modification of a value system in which a woman is expected to bear as many sons as possible for her husband, whose own ego is involved in the number of which he can boast. As a married woman, she must modify her behavior towards her husband and learn how to deal with the family planning consultants—which calls for a role repertoire she may not already possess. In carrying out contraceptive practices, she may feel that she is going against the norms not only of her religion but of some of her neighbors as well. These must be weighed against the supposed economic and psychological benefits of planning the coming of children. In addition, the use of a contraceptive device or pill makes one dependent upon some outside source of supply, even if it is provided at a nominal cost. Thus, to ask a couple to employ inventions from the city to supplant traditional, less effective means of birth control is to ask them to become part of the urban orientation toward desirable family size, toward considera-

3. *Ibid.*, p. 246. Also see J. R. Rele, "Trends and Differentials in the American Age at Marriage," *Milbank Memorial Fund Quarterly*, **43** (April 1968) pp. 219–34.

4. Chukwudum Uche, "Population Problems and Family Planning in Africa," *Sociologia Ruralis*, **12** (1972); 419–430. Also see Karen A. Miller and Alex Inkeles, "Modernity and Acceptance of Family Limitation in Four Developing Countries," *Journal of Social Issues* **30** (1974): 167–88 which stresses need to change individual attitudes.

Table 7–1   Traditional Family Network and Family Planning Network

	TRADITIONAL FAMILY	FAMILY PLANNING NETWORK
Status*	Wife	Family Planning Expert (Public Health Nurse)
Values	More children, more security for parents	More children, less economic security for each child
	Child's arrival is God's will	Births should be planned
	A good wife pleases husband who may not like family planning	Woman's own welfare as important as that of husband
Behavior (Roles)	Use some folk remedies to avoid conception	Should use scientifically proven methods regularly
	Never discuss "sex" with husband	Mates should talk over number of children desired; then limit births
Norms	Husband has sex "rights" which wife cannot deny; recognized in customary law	Wife also has rights recognized in governmental family planning programs
	Religious sanctions against those using birth control	Tax system favors small rather than large families (some countries)

Degrees of articulation: Wife may accept family planning *values,* but not go so far as to carry out family planning roles; wife may practice family planning (roles) because of pressures from husband or others but still hold to traditional values (experiencing feelings of guilt); wife may practice family planning roles despite opposing norms because of her interest in welfare of her children.

*Only two statuses are used here as illustration, though both networks contain additional statuses.

tions about the health of the mother in contrast to the culturally-prescribed ego needs of the father, and to the acceptance of modern scientific values in place of the conventional folk values.

Much the same kind of articulation occurs as mothers participate in well-baby clinics or in other efforts to improve the health of mother and children. The whole setting is somewhat foreign to rural life. The professionals though perhaps rural in origin are likely to be urban-oriented. Carrying out the instructions received may bring the mother into conflict with the older people in the home (say, her mother-in-law) or some influential neighbor.

The Larger Kinship Group and Rural-Urban Contacts

Even where the size of households in rural areas approaches that of urban centers, the bonds between relatives living in separate places may remain strong.[5] To a great degree, this is a cultural trait since in some countries the individual accepts the fact that he cannot achieve very much (e.g., educational attainment) without the backing of his family; in turn, he is ready to help others related to him since he was helped at an earlier point in time. In the case of the Philippines, Tagumpay-Castillo and Pua see definite indications that extended patterns of help and family identification exist when relatives move to other parts of the country. Since most Filipinos rarely move out of a sense of economic necessity but rather because of a desire for economic improvement, they rely upon family communications to bridge the geographic distance between the migrant and his family. Ties remain intact despite absence of face-to-face contact.[6]

Apart from the obvious exchange of economic goods (money, food, etc.) among rural-urban kin, there are important elements modifying the traditional family in the direction of urban values. One has only to point out that the young person in the rural areas finds some relative in the city a more exciting role model than his counterpart in the rural area. Sometimes the authority of the father on the farm is weakened when the father's younger brother makes a successful transition to the city and then comes back for a visit. The sons may want to become more like their uncle than like their father. Or, the girls in the family may begin to emulate the older sister who has gone to the city instead of the women remaining in the village. The changes occurring in the rural family itself under accelerating contact with urban kinsmen have been well documented for many countries. Yet, not all migrants to the city succeed; some merely eke out an existence and thereby have less influence than those much more successful.

Table 7–2 shows interaction between a rural family already in transition from the traditional pattern and the urban kin group still partly traditional in outlook—not completely "urbanized."

The young person who comes to the city to study or work lives or maintains close contact with relatives already there. They, rather than the adults left behind, become his guides; he observes their speech, dress, deportment, and sense of priorities. Thus in a familial context, he is at

5.   In fact the isolation of even the nuclear family has been exaggerated according to recent studies. See John Mogey, *op. cit.*

6.   Gelia Tagumpay-Castillo and Juanita F. Pua, "Research Notes on the Contemporary Filipino Family: Findings in a Tagalog Area," *Philippine Journal of Home Economics*, **14** (July–September 1963), pp. 4–35.

Table 7–2   Rural Family and Urban Kin Group

STATUS	RURAL FAMILY (In Transition)	URBAN KIN GROUP (Partly Traditional)
Values	Education for children	Loyalty to kin group in village
	Some migration, so those remaining have sufficient land base	Security based on rural connections (for food, etc.)
	Some urban conveniences	Prestige accorded by village groups upon return visits
Roles (behavior patterns)	Send son or daughter to city	Receive family member from village; help him/her find a job or school; train him/her into urban ways
	Provide food products to urban kin	Do various favors for rural relatives (e.g., getting government documents)
	Entertain urban kin on feast days	Explain to rural relatives what city life is like; demonstrate by dress and mannerisms
	Care for elderly moving back from the city	Send money back to parents etc., or for improvement of village dwelling, buying more land, etc.
Norms	Attraction for urban ways; weakening controls by neighbors and village public opinion	Employing relatives in own business or in some government agency an accepted norm
	Economic norms outweigh religious and communal standards	Urban regulations about health standards or overcrowding set aside in interest of accommodating relatives

least partially resocialized into a neophyte urbanite.[7] The family has a cushioning effect for the individuals facing traumatic confrontations at

7. Andrei Simic, *The Peasant Urbanites: A Study of Rural-Urban Mobility in Serbia.* New York: The Seminar Press, 1973.

work, with the law, and with the *savoir-faire* of the city people encountered each day.

Thus the family itself, particularly where migration has occurred, becomes a major articulating mechanism between the country and the city, often serving as a "transmission belt."[8]

One final point about the extended family deserves attention. This is the tendency of people in developing countries to favor their relatives when making personnel selections for government or business. For such people, this is the normal, the expected thing. Not to favor one's relatives would mean that one was not a good member of the family; neighbors would lose respect for such an unfilial person.

This is why many rural people are dismayed when foreign experts in the name of modernization advocate policies in which family considerations play no part in selection. The urbanized experts are urging that universalistic criteria (which are available to all people, in theory at least) be substituted for particularistic criteria (which only relatively few people can meet on the basis of kinship, religion, race, caste, or class, etc.).

In the West, procedures have been set up to reduce the favoritism toward relatives, especially in government. To violate this principle is to practice *nepotism*, a term derived from the Latin word *nepos*, or nephew. Despite such rules, however, family considerations tend to permeate choices in all kinds of societies, Western or non-Western. In the West, if one were to employ a nephew in preference to a more qualified person, one would be conscious of breaking a rule and be embarrassed in doing so; elsewhere, where familistic values predominate, there is no sense of guilt but rather a sense of achievement if one finds a job for a relative. This means one has selected someone who can be trusted. A nonrelative would not have the same loyalty, which is very important if one is seeking and consolidating a power base in the community or in society at large.[9]

Contacts with the Legal System

The highly developed legal system of the cities stands in marked contrast to the customary law of traditional societies. The purposes are

8. Ernestine Friedl, "The Role of Kinship in the Transmission of National Culture to Rural Villages in Mainland Greece," *American Anthropologist*, **62** (February 1959): 1, pp. 30–38. Murray A. Straus, "Social Class and Farm-City Differences in Interaction with Kin in Relation to Societal Modernization," *Rural Sociology*, **34** (1969); 476–95.

9. Marion J. Levy, Jr., *Modernization and the Structure of Societies: A Setting for International Affairs*, Vol. Two, Princeton, N.J.: Princeton University Press. 1966, pp. 388–390. Also see Fred W. Riggs, *Administration in Developing Countries: The Theory of Prismatic Society*, Boston: Houghton Mifflin, 1964, pp. 230–31, 272–73.

the same: resolution of conflict, administration of justice, and punishment of offenders against the welfare of the group. Customary law, as opposed to statute law, is embedded in a familistic setting in which individuals are dealt with as persons. The elders sitting in judgment know much about the offenders' family background and guide their decisions accordingly. Frequently rural people first come into contact with the urban-located legal system when they have a dispute over land, especially the division of land among heirs.[10] This cannot be decided by a local justice of the peace or magistrate, but it has to be taken up in the unique atmosphere of a courtroom, preceded of course by many visits to lawyer's offices. These lawsuits often drag on for years, taking up much of the family income in legal fees, and being the subject of much discussion in the village. Table 7–3 shows aspects of the lawyer relationship as illustrative of interaction between the rural family and legal networks.

The law intrudes, at least from the standpoint of some rural people, when its officers seek to enforce school attendance. Parents may feel that they have need of their son's labor on the farm and place a low evaluation on the kind of instruction given in the local school, thus making themselves liable to breaking the school attendance laws. Other regulations control the standardization and quality of agricultural produce that farmers sell, or obligations they assume in obtaining an agricultural loan. Many more illustrations could be given of ways in which the rural people confront the urban world through the legal system. As they learn to use it to accomplish some important purpose of their own, they and their families become more firmly articulated with the national society.

Patron-Client Relationships

Rural people from time immemorial have sought to offset their precarious existence by working out patterns of mutual aid with others. The larger kinship unit is the most immediate source of such assistance. Beyond this, however, there are arrangements in which a particular family becomes linked to people with influence and power in the larger society, people who are not related by blood. This is known as *patronage*. An example is godparenthood.

Godparenthood.   One culture trait of the Western world associated with Christianity is the godparent-godchild relationship. In brief, this is a fictive or ritual kinship arrangement through which a person or a couple assumes responsibility for the spiritual welfare of another individual.

10.   John W. Cole, *Estate Inheritance in the Italian Alps,* Research Report No. 10, Department of Anthropology, University of Massachusetts (Amherst), December, 1971.

Table 7–3   Rural Family and Urban Legal System

STATUS (for Illustration)	HEAD OF RURAL FAMILY	URBAN LAWYER
Values	Defense of rights	Protection of client plus economic gain
Roles	Explains wrongs in terms of particular personalities	Looks at situation in terms of impersonal, legal statutes
	Follows procedures as prescribed by lawyer in strange surroundings (lawyer's office, court room, government office)	Guides client through legal maze, perhaps giving explanations along the way
	Discusses his lawyer with relatives and friends to see if he is being properly advised	May continue case over protracted period of time
	Pays fees, fines or bribes and/or receives compensation if decision in his favor	May advise client to drop case after much expenditure of funds and time
Norms	Struggle over whether to spend time on case at expense of farm work; may be subject to community criticism	Legal norms dictate procedures; professional norms govern lawyer's conduct supposedly
	Acceptance of urban norms in place of settling grievances by personal means (beating up, destruction of other's property, etc.)	May persuade court to take customary law (as well as statutory law) into account in making judicial decisions

The chief occasions where this relationship may come into existence are the rites of Christian baptism and marriage. Elaborate customs govern the behavior of godparents and godchildren toward each other, including the exchange of gifts and decorous behavior (no swearing) in the presence of each other.

Of even more importance from the standpoint of social articulation is the relationship between the godparents and the parents of the godchild. They become related in a spiritual sense and address each other in formal, prescribed ways. Members of the two families may not intermarry. A father may select different godparents for each child, thus entering into this particular relationship with several families. Although the godparent's primary responsibility is to the child, the father of the child can expect a reasonably immediate and positive response when he goes to a godparent for a favor that he rather than the godchild requires. In describing the traditional society of Western Europe, Anderson mentions the survival of godparenthood particularly in Orthodox and Roman Catholic areas to the south and east.

> There, an individual still customarily builds numerous and complex relationships to provide sources of aid when he is in need—when hungry, impoverished, in trouble with a hostile government, or simply looking for a job.[11]

One of the most detailed studies of these patronage relationships has been done for a shepherd group in Greece—the Sarakatsani. Although these shepherds are in frequent conflict with the farmers who live in settled villages, their efforts to link with people outside their immediate group would be similar to the efforts made by the agriculturalists.

> To protect himself the Sarakatsanos tries to establish some kind of link which will transform an otherwise impersonal confrontation into a personal relation: that is, he attempts to draw the individual whose goodwill he wishes to influence into an institutionalized relationship which may exist across the frontiers of community. . . . The most effective means of achieving these ends is the form of spiritual kinship between the bridegroom and his wedding sponsor. . . . After the birth of a child this changes into the even more significant relation between the natural parent and the spiritual parent.[12]

The articulating function of this arrangement is shown by the fact that over half of the ties are with people outside the village studied. "They include cheese merchants, animal dealers, village presidents, members of village councils, village shopkeepers, other prominent villagers with influence, transport lorry owners, veterinary experts, lawyers, Members of Parliament, grammar school teachers, tailors, and others. They have one quality in common that they are able in different ways to help or hinder the families who wish to establish a link of spiritual kinship with them."[13]

The custom of godparenthood was introduced to the New World

---

11. Robert T. Anderson, *Traditional Europe: A Study in Anthropology and History.* Belmont, California: Wadsworth Publishing Company, 1971, pp. 146–47.

12. J. K. Campbell, *Honour, Family and Patronage: A Study of Institutions and Moral Values in a Greek Mountain Community,* Oxford: Clarendon Press, 1964, p. 222.

13. *Ibid.,* p. 223. Also see Dwight B. Heath, "New Patrons for Old: Changing Patron-Client Relationships in the Bolivian Yungas," in A. Strickon and S. M. Greenfield, *Structure and Process in Latin-America: Patronage, Clientage and Power Systems.* Albuquerque: University of New Mexico Press, 1972, pp. 101–137.

with the spread of Christianity by Spanish missionaries. In Mexico, and other Spanish-speaking areas, it is known as *compadrazgo*. There it, too, serves to cement commercial and other ties. A study of one Mexican village shows that in former years the muleteers from this village carried pottery on journeys that lasted sometimes up to a month. "They tried to establish compadrazgo relationships in each town where they stayed so as to have a place to pass the night and a support in case of trouble with local authorities."[14] Such muleteering is a thing of the past but the potters of the village now have compadrazgo ties with urban pottery merchants to whom they deliver most of their wares.

In Mexico, as in Greece, this arrangement offers almost unlimited manipulative opportunities.

> Unlike kinship, an individual has a good deal of control over who is and who is not a compadre; he can consciously seek out those relationships which, whatever the reason, he sees as meaningful. Almost everyone, to some extent, appears to use the compadrazgo to strengthen or solidify position within the community, but some make much more conscious use of the manipulative possibilities than do others.[15]

Although most members of this village have compadrazgo relationships with others in the same village, a few try to enlist as compadres people of superior social and economic status. Lawyers are frequently sought in this connection.

One may well ask what the godparent gets out of this relationship, particularly if he lives outside the community where his godchild resides. First, there is the ego-involvement. It is considered an honor to be asked. The godparent is always given the seat of honor at ceremonial functions and on designated holidays he receives gifts from the godchild (or his parents). Second, there is some reciprocity in the arrangement. Those who seek public office expect support from the families with whom they have godparent ties. Or, if one lives in a city, the village family may prove a source of food at regular intervals. Yet, the obligations of the godparent are real also. In some countries he is expected to underwrite much of the cost of the wedding ceremony and also to help the godchild in time of need.

Of sociological interest is the fact that as far back as the Middle Ages, rural people built into the godparent-godchild relationship a means of support outside the kinship group and, with the passing of time, used this relationship for manipulative purposes in cementing ties outside the village.

14. George M. Foster, *Tzintzuntzan: Mexican Peasants in a Changing World*, Boston: Little, Brown and Company, 1967, p. 81.

15. *Ibid.*, p. 82.

Needless to say, in areas where godparenthood does not exist or is no longer effective—as in most areas outside of Europe and Latin America—more reliance must be placed on one's own kinship group. In traditional China, for instance, the clan—with its requirement of mutual support—included those distantly related by blood but descendants of a common ancestor. In other areas, membership in a common tribe may impose obligations, particularly in an alien environment, such as a city or a mining camp.

Part-Time Farmers and Social Change

Another link between the rural family and the larger society, and the last to be discussed here, is the part-time farmer who, though living on a farm, works off the farm at some nonagricultural job. In the United States, a family is designated "part-time farming" when the farm operator (usually head of the family) works off the farm 100 or more days during the year, or when the nonfarm income of the family exceeds the value of farm products sold. In other countries, different definitions may be used. For example, in areas of traditional agriculture, those who commute daily to an off-farm job are called "peasant-workers" and constitute a significant proportion of the unskilled labor pool. In this case, the family does not migrate, but maintains a land base. Table 7–4 shows competing roles faced by the part-time farmer.

Part-time farming is often studied from the economic standpoint: the number of workers made available for industrialization, the shifting income pattern, and the problems posed for systems of public transportation. Here, however, we focus upon the articulation these workers provide between the rural and urban areas. Several points listed in Table 7–4 can be emphasized:

1. Part-time farming becomes possible with increasing economic opportunities. Rural areas have always had some people who supplemented farm income by serving in off-seasons as teamsters or unskilled workers on roads and nearby construction, though the number was relatively small. With industrialization, and particularly with the location of factories in outlying rural areas, the possibility of nonfarm employment is greatly enhanced.

2. The emphasis upon cash income is increased. One of the appeals of off-farm work is that one is paid in cash, which can then be used to purchase objects connected with a rise in living standards. The part-time farmers see these in the city, buy them, and bring them home, and they are then emulated by neighbors and fellow-villagers.

3. The farm work is left up to the women and the elderly. Since off-farm employment is supplementary to the agricultural enterprise, someone must carry out the farm tasks. The family head is away each day. If his commute is very long, and it often takes two hours each way, he has little

Table 7–4   Competing *Roles* of Part-Time Farmer

TYPE	FARM ROLES	NONFARM ROLES
Economic	Reduces crop acreage or livestock numbers or tries to handle former tasks in evening and on days off from non-farm job.	Performs new occupational skills in return for supplementary cash income.
	May have to pay for extra help, or rely on family members.	Pays out money and spends time in commuting to job.
	Able to make some capital investments on farm with off-farm income.	Talks with fellow-workers, who may represent urban values primarily.
	May learn about new farming methods and secure supplies in locality where he works, or may lose interest in maximizing returns from his farm.	Becomes more aware of differences in rural-urban living standards.
Sociological	Less time with family; leaves many daily decisions up to wife and others.	Caught in confusion as to occupational identity.
	Less involved in community affairs because of less time and shifting interest.	Shift in recreational pursuits, more of which may be satisfied in city.
	Advice may be more frequently sought if he becomes "gatekeeper" to non-rural jobs.	

time to devote to farming. Therefore, his wife and other adults (parents, aunts, etc.) living with him must do the farming. Children are also involved. Studies in Eastern Europe show that most of the peasant-workers come from the smaller farms, but even so, the labor required for a small farm is considerable at the peak periods.[16]

4. The part-time farmer forms new associations at work that may lead to different leisure-time activities, new political views, and certainly greater desire for economic improvement. These changes may conflict with those of family members and others who have remained in full-time farming. They go beyond the acquisition of material goods (television, city suit, or motorcycle) to modifications in behavior patterns themselves.

16. Walter C. Bisselle, "Peasant-Workers in Poland," (pp. 79–90) and William G. Lockwood, "The Peasant-Worker in Yugoslavia," (pp. 91–110) *Studies in European Society*, Vol. 1 (July 1973). Whole issue devoted to The Workers-Peasants in Europe.

5. A new conception of oneself is related to these changed behavior patterns. A man may stop thinking of himself as a peasant or farmer and begin to think of himself as a worker; his dominant focus may become the factory rather than the farm. This can take place even though peasant-workers or part-time farmers as a group may be less well-educated (in the sense of formal schooling) than urban workers.

6. The rural community as a social unit is greatly weakened as a larger proportion of its members become peasant-workers. These workers no longer feel as subject to the local social controls; some of their interests lie elsewhere. Consequently, much deeper social divisions than existed in the past separate those with these different work orientations.

To summarize, the part-time farmer, whether a peasant-worker or some other type, is a conduit for the introduction of urban ways into the rural community. He extends the social networks of the family and has increased linkage through his associations with people outside his village. What he acquires and what he does is observed by those who remain in full-time farming and often influences their desires and self-perceptions.

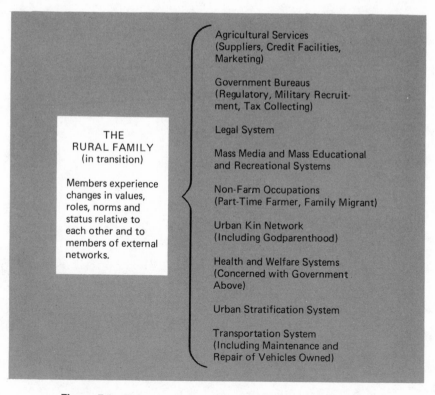

THE
RURAL FAMILY
(in transition)

Members experience
changes in values,
roles, norms and
status relative to
each other and to
members of external
networks.

Agricultural Services
(Suppliers, Credit Facilities,
Marketing)

Government Bureaus
(Regulatory, Military Recruitment, Tax Collecting)

Legal System

Mass Media and Mass Educational
and Recreational Systems

Non-Farm Occupations
(Part-Time Farmer, Family Migrant)

Urban Kin Network
(Including Godparenthood)

Health and Welfare Systems
(Concerned with Government
Above)

Urban Stratification System

Transportation System
(Including Maintenance and
Repair of Vehicles Owned)

Figure 7-1   The rural family and illustrative external networks

Such agents of change need not be only men, for many women—married and unmarried—also engage in work off the farm. Though efforts are made to keep them in a more sheltered environment the contrasts in freedom away from and within the village are quite marked.

To describe even a few of the ways in which rural families articulate with the rural society is difficult for so many lines of contact emanate from the family, the central institution of a rural society. Figure 7-1 reviews some that are most obvious. Those that have been discussed include: networks connected with demographic concerns; the interaction within a far-flung larger kinship group; contacts with a legal system at times running counter to customary village law; patron-client relationships; and, finally, part-time farming. Others, such as recreational and educational systems, will be taken up in later chapters. Certainly, rural families are caught up in the flux of social change, with broadening and deepening of contacts with the larger society.

CHAPTER 8
RELIGION, CHANGING SOCIAL VALUES, AND ARTICULATION

Rural people, particularly in the nonindustrialized countries, organize their lives around a set of social values almost exclusively reflecting a religious orientation. With industrialization, a number of secular values become a part of the overall value system: economic values such as efficiency and success; political values such as independence, individual rights, and democracy; scientific values such as objectivity and rationality. Therefore, one of the first aspects of religion we shall discuss is religious orientation and its connection with the values of rural people. Then, we shall consider the role of religious ritual and ceremony as forms of expressive behavior in rural communities. Third, we shall examine religion as a social organization in terms of the social networks linking rural people to the nonrural segment of their society.

RELIGIOUS ORIENTATIONS AND VALUE SYSTEMS

One function of religion is to provide a set of explanations about the nature of man, the universe, the problem of suffering, and the meaning of human existence. Such explanations constitute a system of readymade beliefs for those who accept it and wish to use it to face life's problems. Each of the major world religions—Islam, Hinduism, Buddhism, Judaism, Christianity, Confucianism—contains such a system of explanations.

In addition, the major religions have developed a set of priorities or emphases, that should characterize social conduct. These go beyond the ethical standards of what is right and wrong to include the chief values to be stressed in society. Although such values are often given a sacred character because they were enunciated by the major prophet or religious leader and are contained in the scriptures, we should remember that cultural values as used in social science are abstractions by an observer. They are based on the observation of certain similarities in the way groups of people behave, either in different situations or over time, or both. Thus we base a description of the dominant values of a society on observed behavior (including what people say), even though the behavior may not conform precisely to the priorities set by the teachings of the dominant religions.

One way to illustrate the influence of religious orientations is to relate selected values commonly attributed to rural societies to the teachings of the religion which predominates in the area being described. Some values have already been discussed in earlier chapters. Family loyalty and the willingness of the individual to submerge his own interests into that of the family group were taken up in the last chapter. These are values embodied in the major religions: "Honor thy father and thy mother" is a part of the Judaeo-Christian tradition and filial piety (respect for parents and elders) is one of the cornerstones of Confucianism. Land and its ownership is another value that has been stressed. At one extreme are those rural people who consider the earth holy and the soil under their control a sacred trust. This emphasis predates most major religions and goes back to an earlier epoch where earth goddesses and fertility divinities were worshiped. Some rural people, for economic rather than religious reasons, place a high value on land ownership, and are ready to treat it instrumentally as a factor in production rather than as a sacred trust not to be bought or sold. Yet, they still value land.

Conservatism is another value associated with rural living. The roots of conservatism vary greatly from one rural society to another, at times simply implying a loyalty to traditions or at other times resistance to almost any type of innovation. Insight into one kind of conservatism and its relationship to a major religion (Islam) is afforded by a description of a Jordanian village.[1]

Kufr al-Ma is a cereal-growing village in the denuded Eastern foothills of the Jordan Valley. Its population of 2,000 is composed entirely of Sunni Moslems. Although many changes occurred in the village, such as land reform, it still is socially conservative. For example, there is no

1. Richard T. Antoun, "Conservatism and Change in the Village Community: A Jordanian Case Study." Reproduced by permission of the Society for Applied Anthropology from *Human Organization*, **24** (Spring, 1965), pp. 4–10.

class system; social status differences are insignificant despite the presence of a number of affluent members of the community, most of whom are engaged in nonagricultural pursuits based on contacts outside the village. Why does the village remain so egalitarian when one would expect its people to divide along economic lines?

In answering this question, Richard T. Antoun listed some variables that play a part. First, those in agriculture are in subsistence farming and have little surplus that would set one family apart from another; those who work outside the village—and men have done this for decades—cannot commute easily and so the nucleus of an upper class in the village (clerks, army officers, school teachers) is not present since these people with distinctive life styles are drawn outside the community. Second, because of the "multiplex" social ties, those ties that serve many interests, people are caught up in a wide network of social relationships. Since these are multisided (economic, religious, political, consanguineal, or recreational), they become tinged with moral and ethical meaning. As a result even those who work outside the village still feel bound morally to those in the village and maintain their village orientation even while away. The prestige structure is such that they would bring disgrace on their family if they violated the norms of the village, so they continue to subscribe to the local values.

An important variable closely linked to the above is the ideological commitment provided by Islam itself.

The absence of incipient stratification in the presence of substantial economic differentiation cannot, however, be wholly explained by circumstances particular to the village of Kufr al-Ma. Reference must be made to Islam, the prevailing ideology of peasant villages in the entire Middle East. Islam preaches a universalistic norm. That is, all men are to be treated by the same standard. A tradition of the Prophet states.

> There is no distinction in religion
> except as to piety.

Islam does not support equalization of wealth between all believers, and the Quran explicitly states,

> As to the means of sustenance, God
> has preferred some of you to others. . . .

Still, the Islamic ethic strongly supports norms of generosity, hospitality, and charity. The zakat, or alms-due, is a pillar of the faith. The show of hospitality on social occasions (such as marriage, funeral, circumcision, and completion of house-building) is customary. During the holy month of Ramadan, village-wide visiting and sharing of meals, particularly with the poor, is common. The day-to-day superordinate-subordinate relationship that prevails between a daily agricultural wage laborer and his employer is modified by social relations of a more friendly and informal sort. The men of the wealthiest and most respected families plow land and quarry rock alongside the laborer they have hired.

The Islamic ethic coincides with and supports certain local customs. A traditional and continuing means of achieving status is the investment in sheep which are slaughtered for honored guests and kinsmen on appropriate occasions. Visitors who pass through Kufr al-Ma and wish to spend the night there are always referred to the richest men in the village, men who can offer good meals and proper sleeping accommodations. By doing so they 'curtain the village,' preserving its reputation for hospitality and adding to their own prestige. The traditional mode of status accumulation, then, has built within it the tendency toward dispersion of wealth. Such a system softens the results of economic differentiation.[2]

Kufr al-Ma is not a typical Moslem village, for no village could be typical of the Moslem world. But it does show how resistance to one kind of change—namely, increased stratification—is based on the religious orientation of its inhabitants.

Two other values often found together are submission to nature and the leisurely approach to time. The Algerian peasant illustrates these, as shown in a study of the Kabyles, who are Berber-speaking with a strong Arab admixture. Their attitudes "are expressions of the traditional values of Islam: the decorum which frowns upon haste, the respect for personalities, the priority of kinship ties over abstract principles of economic and juridical relations, and an attitude towards the future which the West, with perhaps an inadequate awareness of its own dogmas in this regard, qualifies by the epithet of 'fatalist.' "[3]

Selected observations concerning the Kabyles include:

Submission to nature is inseparable from submission to the passage of time scanned in the rhythms of nature. The profound feelings of dependence and solidarity toward that nature whose vagaries and rigours he suffers, together with the rhythms and constraints to which he feels the more subject since his techniques are particularly precarious, foster in the Kabyle peasant an attitude of submission and of nonchalant indifference to the passage of time which no one dreams of mastering, using up, or saving. The refined courtesy of the Kabyle, the courtesy of a man of leisure, is characterized by the same indifference to time. All the acts of life are free from the limitations of the timetable, even sleep, even work which ignores all obsession with productivity and yields. Haste is seen as a lack of decorum combined with diabolical ambition.[4]

... Indifference with regard to punctuality appears in all kinds of behavior. There are not precise hours for meals; they are eaten whenever the preparation is complete and eating is leisurely. The notion of an exact appointment

2. Ibid., p. 7.

3. Julian Pitt-Rivers (ed.), Mediterranean Countrymen: Essays in the Social Anthropology of the Mediterranean. Paris: Mouton, 1963, p. 14.

4. Pierre Bourdieu, "The Attitude of the Algerian Peasant Toward Time," in Julian Pitt-Rivers (ed.), supra, p. 57.

is unknown; they agree only to meet 'at the next market.' In the cities women are often seen waiting at the hospital or before the doctor's office two or three hours before it is due to open.

Time stretches out, given a rhythm by the round of work and holidays and by the succession of nights and days. Time so marked is not, as has often been shown, measured time.[5]

In contrast to this orientation toward nature and time, we find other farmers—particularly in the Western world—who value mastery over nature, though at times this can be a losing battle as experience with the Dust Bowl in the United States in the 1930's has shown.

Fatalism is another value ascribed to rural people, particularly in the Middle East and Asia, where it supposedly reflects the religious orientations dominant in those areas. It is important, however, to distinguish between different kinds of fatalism, although all types seem to grow out of an inability to control events.[6] On the basis of an analysis of 57 case histories of efforts by outsiders to introduce changes in rural areas, Niehoff and Anderson recognize that most supernatural systems of thought do contain fatalistic beliefs of some sort, but these need not be insurmountable barriers to social change. This is because there is a gap between what people profess to believe and what they actually do. In fact, the clergy try to narrow this gap in their efforts to persuade people to approximate more closely in their conduct the ideals of their faith. The authors note:

If, in fact, people say that their destiny is established the moment they are born, but contradict this by actions which are directed toward improving the conditions of their lives, then the fatalism which they believe controls their lives is not an absolutely limiting factor for change.[7]

A study of the heads of poor families in the Mississippi Delta gives further support for this point of view. It shows a connection between fatalism and poverty, but it also finds that these do not affect an individual's mobility potential. "There is no support for the notion that apathy or fatalism makes those in the lower strata resist change."[8]

To summarize, many values are attributed to rural societies. At

5. *Ibid.*, p. 59.

6. Arthur H. Niehoff and J. Charnel Anderson, "Peasant Fatalism and Socioeconomic Innovation," *Human Organization*, **25** (Winter, 1966), pp. 273–83.

7. *Ibid.*, p. 277.

8. C. Hobson Bryan and Alvin L. Bertrand, *Propensity for Change Among the Rural Poor in the Mississippi Delta: A Study of the Roots of Social Mobility*, Agricultural Economic Report No. 185, Economic Research Service, U.S. Department of Agriculture in cooperation with Louisiana State Agricultural Experiment Station, Louisiana State University, p. 21.

times, these are over-idealized by those who see in the peasant or farmer the true repository of national wisdom or the basic virtues modern urban man has "unfortunately lost." Values such as family loyalty, pride in land ownership, conservatism, respect for nature, leisurely approach to time, and fatalism grow out of human experience, and they become sacred as they are embodied in revered scriptures and traditions. The particular set of values and the priorities among them will vary from one rural group to another, but familiarity with them is essential if one is to understand the social world of which they are a part. Table 8–1 lists some of the different "traditional" and "modern" values.

Table 8–1   Selected Traditional Rural Values and Their Opposites

SELECTED TRADITIONAL VALUES	SELECTED "MODERN" VALUES
Family Loyalty	Individual rights
Land ownership as sacred trust	Land as a commodity
Conservatism	Progress
Submission to nature	Mastery over nature
Leisurely approach to time	Efficient use of time
Fatalism	Acceptance of possibility of change and of personal responsibility

Note: Some religions tend to stress primarily the traditional values; other religions emphasize some "modern" values as well, which many rural people today accept.

To point out that the major world religions supply and reinforce values for their adherents is to list only one aspect of the role of these religions. Another function lies in the ceremonies and rituals. Whereas values and beliefs have to do with the knowing or cognitive aspects, ceremonies and rituals deal with the expressive, affective, emotional side of human beings.

CEREMONIES AND RITUALS: EXPRESSIVE BEHAVIOR

Religious observances and ceremonies have been developed to help people deal with life's major crises. There are ceremonies connected with birth, such as those leading to the "purification" of the mother and others to the naming of the child. Baptism and circumcision rituals are found in different faiths, with the former being important among Christians and the latter significant among the Moslems and Jews. Other ceremonies signify growing maturity, such as confirmation in the Catholic church or public ceremonies among tribal groups. Marriage, too, becomes an occasion for widespread public attention and festivity, often being preceded by numerous customary acts involving the giving of a dowry or the purchase of the bride. In any event, the ceremony frequently signifies the joining of two families, not just two individuals.

The wife may resort to ritualized procedures designed to bring about fertility if a marriage does not produce children. These procedures may use magic or may invoke the help of the supreme deity. Also in times of illness affected parties seek religious help, through the services of the religious leader whom they frequently consult before going to anyone trained in Western medicine. When death occurs, religious rites and consolation help the bereaved family adjust to their loss, with some customs often performed to aid the soul of the departed in his afterlife. Urban people, of course, face similar crises and may observe the same rites.

Rural rituals relate not only to the life cycle of the individual but to the annual cycle of the seasons. There are rites carried out at the time of first sowing to ensure a good crop and there are harvest celebrations. In case of drought or flood, sacred objects may be carried through the fields or special prayers may be held in the church, temple, or shrine. Religious holidays punctuate the year and for each of these there are customs that have some bearing upon the agricultural cycle. Where the main religion follows a lunar calendar, as in the case of Islam, the rites come on a different date each year and therefore do not follow the seasons as closely as they do under the Western calendar.

Some rites relate to the supernatural deities worshiped within a major religion whereas other rites are more magical or pragmatic, and they actually may consist of practices which the official religious body would frown upon, such as pre-Christian customs associated with the Christian ceremony of committing the body to the grave and the soul to God.

Mandelbaum shows that there is no antagonism between the transcendantal complex (ultimate, supernal, derived from Sanskrit literature) and the pragmatic complex (proximate, local, validated by vernacular tales) in traditional village life in India. He writes:

> . . . The Brahmin priest does not forbid the propitiation of the local spirits, nor does the shaman's indwelling voice decry the worship of the Sanskritic gods or deny their stringent requirements for ritual purity. The two are complementary, each serving important but differing religious purposes.
>   Both are observed at all levels of the social hierarchy and both contribute to the total religious practice of the village community. The transcendental complex is in the keeping of the higher castes since their men

alone were trained in the study of Sanskrit scripture and in the performance of the more complex rites. . . .

The pragmatic complex is more in the keeping of religious specialists drawn from the lower jatis [an hereditary endogamous caste group], but people of the highest caste rank, especially women, will make offerings at the local shrines, consult shamans, and may even participate in some way in the festivals of the local deities. Hence there is no sharp social division in religious practice; the higher groups do not follow the literate tradition only and the lower jatis only the vernacular complex. There is rather a separation of religious specialists by caste level and a greater intensity of worship of the universalistic, system-maintaining gods by the higher jatis (who do manage the social systems) and of the pragmatic deities by the lower.[9]

These comments indicate the importance of the religious specialist, by whatever title he may be known (Table 8–2).

Festivals also play a significant role in rural communities. Pararin, a Peruvian Andean settlement of 172 houses, is relatively isolated but continues the traditional celebration of holy days despite marked economic changes.

Easter Week (Semana Santa). The festivities on this occasion are both more religious and elaborate than the other minor celebrations. On the five Saturdays preceding Holy Week, the Virgin of the Rosary is taken in procession around the plaza, accompanied by another saint each time.

For Easter week itself, the most "solemn" days are Holy Wednesday, Maundy Thursday, and Good Friday on which days there will be a priest and mass and processions held. There are several special functionaries who have charge of the different events during the week. The *Junta de Fabrica* names a "chorus master" (*maestro de coro* also called *maestro de capilla* or chapel master) each year to contract five or six chanters for the week's ceremonies (mass, processions and evening prayers).

Other functionaries are the two *llaveros,* volunteers who are responsible for adorning the church and images in the church. The *llaveros* are also supposed to offer a public banquet on Maundy Thursday. They also decide to hire a band (usually brought from the town of Llipa in Bolognesi Province) or contract local musicians.

For the processions, four *maverales* take charge of each of the two litters, one bearing Christ and the other, the Virgin Mary. It is expected that they will make the litters "all wax," that is, cover them with candles, for each of the processions.

A final type of official for this festival is the *regidor.* Several may be appointed by the *Junta de Fabrica.* It is the duty of the *regidores* to make the proper invitations to everyone for the banquets which are held.

The processions and masses of Easter are well-attended by the rest

9. David G. Mandelbaum, "Process and Structure in South Asian Religion," *Journal of Asian Studies,* **23** (June 1964).

of the population and the atmosphere is primarily religious rather than recreational.[10]

Table 8–2   Religious Leaders as Articulating Agents

TYPE	FUNCTION	EXAMPLES
1. Reinforcing local values (e.g. Shamans).	Dealing with immediate daily problems of individual families (magical, invoking local deities) (based on vernacular folklore).	Rituals to overcome infertility, illness; blessing a new house; curing Evil Eye.
2. Reinforcing more universalistic values (e.g. Brahmin priests).	Dealing with community problems and public behavior (invoking supernatural deity or deities) (based on sacred scriptures).	Marriages, ceremonies to overcome drought, festivals.
3. Same as (2), but also representing a nationally organized religious body (Catholic priest, Protestant minister).	Maintenance of the faith; gaining new adherents; recruiting likely candidates for the clergy.	Youth and adult conferences, organized religious teaching (Sunday School, e.g.), religious services with a sermon, collections for missionary activities at home and abroad.

Note: In (2) and (3) above the sacred scriptures give a common background for both rural and nonrural adherents of a given religion; in (3) the articulation with the "outside world" is purposely emphasized. Any religious leader in (2) may at times perform at level (1), while a leader in (3) may perform at levels (1) and (2).

The rites and festivals that are a part of the religious system provide not only a prescribed way of meeting certain crises; they also afford occasions to reinforce the sense of community. Special celebrations bring back native sons and daughters from the urban areas and attract many other outsiders as well. In some rural sections of the United States, the annual evangelistic revival services held much the same significance as more traditional festivals elsewhere.

10. Paul L. Doughty and Luis Negron, *Pararin: A Break with the Past,* Socio-Economic Development of Andean Communities Report No. 6. Cornell Peru Project, Cornell University, 1964, pp. 50–51.

RELIGIOUS ORGANIZATION
AND SOCIAL ARTICULATION

By providing an orientation accepted in varying degrees by both rural and urban people, a major religion can help tie the two population segments together. Where farmers and urbanites both share in the traditions of Islam, or of Buddhism, or of Christianity, there is at least an implicit set of shared values, doctrines, and moral standards to be called into play. Of course, where a national population is divided according to two, three, or more major religions, the problem of finding a common basis of action becomes more difficult. Frequently in such cases nationalism or class interests seem to be the only binding force that transcends the religious differences.

Common religious rites and festivals also can have a cohesive influence, particularly where they bring about increased interaction among those who have gone to the city and those who have remained behind in the rural area. Such common observances, along with the upkeep of the place of worship (shrine, temple, church) calls for more than beliefs or expressive behavior: it necessitates at least some social organization. Thus, in all localities we find religious groups, sometimes very informal and sometimes highly organized. The religious leader is a key figure in many of these groups, but he could not be a leader without followers, adherents, and supporters.

Rural sociologists, particularly in the United States, have studied religious groups in the same way they have dealt with other kinds of groups in rural areas. One of the most thorough studies of the rural church was carried out in 1952 in Missouri by the rural sociologists of the University of Missouri (Columbia). In 1957 they published seven research bulletins:

Part I	Introduction
Part II	Rural Religious Groups
Part III	Clergymen in Rural Missouri
Part IV	Index of Religious Group Action
Part V	Rural-Urban Churches Compared
Part VI	Spatial and Social Relationships
Part VII	What Rural People Think of Church

This original study assumes even greater significance because another study of the same 99 rural townships in the United States was conducted 15 years later, in 1967.[11] What changes had occurred?

11.   Edward W. Hassinger and John S. Holik, "Changes in the Number of Rural Churches in Missouri, 1952–1967," *Rural Sociology*, 35 (September 1970), pp. 354–66.

First, of all the number of religious groups (those that held public worship) had not declined as much as one would have anticipated. Table 8–3 gives the figures:

Table 8–3   Gains and Losses in Religious Groups, 1952–1967, By Church Type and Sect Type

GAINS AND LOSSES	CHURCH TYPE	SECT TYPE	TOTAL
Number in 1952	391	143	534
Losses (1952–1967)	47	22	69
Additions (1952–1967)	18	28	46
Number in 1967	362	149	511
Net gain or loss	− 29	+ 6	− 23
Percentage net gain or loss of 1952 base	− 7.4%	+ 4.2%	− 4.3%

Chi-square = 9.4; d.f. = 1; significant at the 5 percent level.

Source: Edward W. Hassinger and John S. Holik, "Changes in the Number of Rural Churches in Missouri, 1952–1967," Rural Sociology, 35 (September 1970), pp. 354–366.

There was a loss of 23 churches, or a drop of 4.3 percent. Most of the decline was in the open country, whereas the large village experienced an increase in congregations.

Second, the table above divides the religious groups into the church-type and the sect-type. The original study stated that the church-type is characterized by the tendency to adjust to the secular society, and the sect-type is characterized by the tendency to withdraw from the secular society. Some illustrations of the church-type are the Southern Baptist Convention, Disciples of Christ, the Protestant Episcopal Church, as well as Methodist, Lutheran, Presbyterian, and Roman Catholic churches. Sect-types include a wide variety such as Freewill Baptists, Pentecostal churches, and Assemblies of God. Whereas the church-type lost congregations to the extent of 7.5 percent in the 15 year period, the sect-type gained 4.2 percent. The major sect-type gains came in the Ozark area, which is agriculturally marginal, with low income and considerable population loss.

A third finding is the expected fact that the demise of religious groups came where the membership had grown very small and so was unable to carry on a program. In these cases, the centralized denominations tended to impose mergers upon the struggling groups, whereas such extra pressures were not present for sect-type groups.

Studies such as these show that in the rural United States religious groups continue to have significance, although statistics show a higher proportion of church members in the urban than rural areas. The church-type, as its definition shows, seeks to adjust to secular society. This does not mean surrendering its principles so much as recognizing that its members are a part of a social world in which religion is one of the forces competing for an individual's time, resources, and loyalty. Table 8–4 seeks

Table 8–4   Activities (Roles) of a Local Congregation* That May Lead to Increased Articulation

EMPLOYING THE MINISTER

May be assigned by bishop or central church office.	Local groups may request a certain type of leader.
May be employed by local congregation itself.	Committee interviews and evaluates candidates for the opening.

Result: The clergy, many brought in from outside, serve as a professional link between local congregation and national church structure.

INSTRUCTION IN THE FAITH

Church Service	A feature is the sermon, in which minister may deal with issues of broad national concern. Guest ministers may also do this.
Sunday School	Use of teaching materials prepared in urban, national headquarters by trained specialists, who often include ideas and illustrations (e.g. race relations) that may run counter to local values in the rural community.
Special Study Groups	Various church organizations in search of speakers and programs may invite those whose presentations broaden horizons.
Church Conferences	Meet people from other communities, listen to speakers with a national reputation, report back to local church group on experience.

Result: Through speakers and printed materials urban values and norms may be disseminated.

PROMOTING CHURCH "CAUSES'

Financial drives for home missions and foreign missions.	For every such drive special appeals are made (often in form of printed material) that describe activities of national church organization and need for support.

Result: Members become aware of participation in a wider community than that of their local parish, though sometimes developing incorrect stereotypes of the people to be helped.

Table 8–4 (cont.)

SHARING LOCAL COMMUNITY CONCERNS

Shared activity with other religious groups in same community (union services, fellowship breakfast).	Association with church groups more articulated into the national society than one's own may shift one's perspectives (e.g. some churches serve wine at church functions, others do not; some dance, others do not).
Shared activity with secular groups (encouraging support for various financial drives, environmental programs, community events, etc.).	May lead to controversy where community opinion is divided on an issue or as to role a church should play in secular affairs.

Result: Members may occasionally be required to test their preconceived notions against the hard reality of notions held by other people.

IDENTIFICATION WITH THE NATION

Prayers for national leaders.	Hope expressed that national leaders will uphold morality and provide leadership in keeping with teachings of church.
Display of flag and commemoration of national holidays.	Associating church and national symbols implies a common interest.
Support for "our side" in terms of war or the reverse: questioning the waging of war itself.	Reaction to war often crystallized by personal views of minister, which may or may not receive majority support among members.

Result: Adherence to the national ethos and involvement in patriotic activities may transmit or contradict the religious teachings, or at least at times make them seem of secondary importance.

*Pattern used here for illustration is the *church* and not *sect;* rural Protestant rather than rural Catholic, including village churches and not only "open country" ones. It is recognized, of course, that sometimes these tendencies work in reverse and may reinforce parochialism rather than articulation.

to trace activities (roles) of a local church-type Protestant congregation in an effort to show the possible ways affiliation with such a local church group might lead to greater articulation external to the community. The table includes only illustrative activities. It should be recognized that no single individual is influenced to feel more of a part of the national society by all activities and many individuals are not influenced by any. But the network of the church can nevertheless be a facilitating mechanism.

The church-type groups tend to have trained clergy who have been prepared in a theological seminary and who are affiliated with other

clergymen. They also promote the use of the special Sunday School materials prepared by the denominational headquarters. These materials usually reflect religion in a broad, world-wide setting. Such clergymen also
explain and solicit funds for the various causes financed by the denomination's home and foreign missions, for care of the needy, and, at times, for
social issues of a controversial nature. Young people are urged to attend
conferences and are assisted in the conduct of their local youth groups
in the church. Therefore, even in denominations such as the Baptists,
where great responsibility devolves upon the local congregation, there is
an awareness of overall denominational activity and a sense of being part
of a large organization seeking to advance a particular religious point of
view and specified religious practices. In the church-type group, members
are exhorted in various ways to try to change their social environment,
to make it more Christian in character and to make themselves a witness
to their religious convictions.

The sect-type groups may bring about articulation not so much by
helping their members take on secular values as by giving them a sense
of separation, of being a special group that is spiritually superior to other
religious groups that temporize with the world. This feeling of spiritual
superiority can help many people face what they consider a hostile world
and can offset the effects of inferior education, income, and general social
standing. This separateness can create fellowship with those in their religious group, which can mean much in an impersonal unfriendly world.
Studies of some highly emotional sects show that on occasion they become
outlets for emotions that otherwise would cause revolts against authority
either in the form of labor disputes or political dissatisfaction.

Other studies of rural areas in the United States have shown the
positive relationship in one denomination between high church activity
and the desire for higher education among young people;[12] the greater
conservatism in civil rights attitudes of church leaders in rural areas in
comparison with those in nonrural areas;[13] and the greater tendency for
rural people who work off the farm to affiliate with village and town
churches.[14] None of these findings is very surprising, but they do illustrate
the need to include the study of religious groups in any comprehensive
account of rural life in the United States. The special problems of the

12.   John R. Christiansen, John W. Payne, and Kenneth J. Brown, "Church Participation and College Desires of Rural Youth in Utah," *Rural Sociology*, **28** (June
1963), pp. 176–85.

13.   Hart M. Nelson and Raytha L. Yokley, "Civil Rights Attitudes of Rural and
Urban Presbyterians," *Rural Sociology*, **35** (June 1970), pp. 161–74.

14.   Ramon E. Henkel and Glenn V. Fuguitt, "Nonfarm Work and the Social Relationships of Farmers," *Rural Sociology*, **31** (March 1966), pp. 80–88.

rural church become only too clear in this period of rapid social change. These problems are: slow adaptation to change because each ethnic group wished to have its own church carried over from Europe, with the weakness that such divisions imply; too many churches for a declining rural population; the shortage of rural ministers; inadequate programs; and inadequate finances.[15]

To conclude, social articulation through religious networks occurs as the local religious group becomes more closely tied to the national headquarters of that group in ways that have just been described. Articulation may also be viewed in terms of the secularization process, which describes the substitution by members of the society of secular (modern) values for the sacred (traditional) values.[16] The secular values stress rationality as a means to accomplish desired goals rather than reliance upon revelation or authority. Of course, not all sacred values are necessarily religious but they are not supposed to be questioned.

The interpretation of the role played by religious bodies in social articulation is subject to one's philosophical assumptions about the nature of society and one's theory of social change. The equilibrium point of view tends to ascribe a positive contribution to religion in terms of the functions described above, while recognizing that there are numerous cases where religious structures have become dysfunctional for the achievement of goals set by national leaders. The conflict point of view tends to discount the importance of religion, viewing it at times as an exploitive institution working in the interests of privileged groups. Certainly, cases can be cited where this is true. It is of sociological interest to note, however, that some of the more fervent supporters of the conflict school substitute a political "religion" for traditional religion in their lives. This "political" religion has its scriptures, its apostles, its sacred, unquestioning acceptance of the authority of a political party, and its symbols for which supreme sacrifices are to be made.

15.   Robert L. Skrabanek, "The Rural Church: Characteristics and Problems," in Alvin L. Bertrand (ed.), *Rural Sociology: An Analysis of Contemporary Rural Life*, New York: McGraw-Hill, 1958, pp. 237–52.

16.   See Henri Mendras, *The Vanishing Peasant: Innovation and Change in French Agriculture*, Cambridge, Mass.: The MIT Press, 1970, pp. 89, 208–10; Howard Becker, "Current Sacred-Secular Theory and its Development," in Howard Becker and Alvin Boskoff (eds.), *Modern Sociological Theory in Continuity and Change*, New York: The Dryden Press, 1957, pp. 133–185; Victor Stoltzfus, "Amish Agriculture: Adaptive Strategies for Economic Survival of Community Life," *Rural Sociology*, **38** (Summer 1973), p. 199.

CHAPTER 9
EDUCATION
OF
THE YOUNG

Education can be a channel to improved social status and entry to non-farm occupations for the individual in a rural society. Parents value education and its articulation with urban ways to the extent that they want their children to move off the farm.

Economists, who also value education, provide a second perspective. They speak of manpower or human resources and indicate that a literate, educated labor force is necessary for industrialization. At the same time, economists also recognize that some countries have trained thousands for jobs that do not exist and filled them with expectations that cannot be realized. The unemployed intellectual cannot assume a lesser position without his own loss of face and that of his relatives. The stress in this second perspective is more upon training in skills than in the classical heritage or liberal arts tradition.

Those interested in political integration provide a third perspective. They view the educational system as a means of inculcating nationalistic values into rural youngsters whose parents may have little conception of nationhood or citizenship. Thus, they hope education will eventually weld the rural sector more firmly to the larger society.

Education, however, need not be associated only with the young. Adults need basic education and advanced education. This applies particularly to farm families whose cooperation is sought in agricultural and home-improvement programs. Such persons are urged to accept more efficient practices not only to increase their own income and raise their standard of living, but to supply national needs in food and other agricultural products. This is especially important for a large number of nations whose agricultural exports account for 40 to 50 percent of their foreign trade. Thus, rural adults, regardless of their attitude toward the education of their children, become the targets of educational programs "to help them," which are designed by planners and others concerned with national goals. The purpose of such programs is change, and change away from traditional agriculture.

Therefore, in considering education as a force in rural society we will first see how knowledge is transmitted in a traditional society through informal education; then we can see what rural schooling is really like and how the countryside and the city differ in educational attainment and quality of instruction. In the next chapter, we can take a critical look at the role of education in national development, including educational programs aimed at adults.

INFORMAL EDUCATION
IN RURAL SOCIETIES

Informal education occurs within a well-defined social network. The status of *teacher* is filled by parents, kinfolk, neighbors, and others in the community. These informal teachers may be adults or even the learner's peers, since many behavior patterns can be taught by those just a little older than the learner. While a youngster is being shown *what* to do in a given situation and *how* to do it, he is also being taught the values surrounding the behavior (why it is important and why it must be done in the appropriate way). He also learns the norms, the rewards and penalties, for right and wrong behavior, for efficient and inefficient techniques. As he grows up, the child learns that there are deviant individuals in the community. They do not farm, keep house, or deport themselves as do the majority of people in the community. They may be deviant in that they drink too much, are lazy, disrespectful, or sexually immoral; or they may be deviant because they are too advanced in the innovations they introduce from outside. Often, such deviants become an important part of the informal education network, either because they are held up as horrible examples or because they hold an attraction to the young.

When schools were introduced into the rural community, especially under a national system of education, people were faced with a different approach to learning. Formal schooling was primarily prescriptive: the teacher and the textbooks told and explained, admonished, and exhorted. Such schooling made little use of demonstration or of participation, thereby seeming much less effective than the informal learning.

Schools also seemed in competition with the family in the early days. The Polish sociologist Boguslaw Galeski notes this:

In peasant farming, as a young man grows up he also gains the general experience necessary for carrying on the operation of the farm. Distinct functions are linked to different ages, and the boy or girl performs these functions within the limits of the family economy, passing in turn through all the stages and preparing him or herself for the future role of farmer or farmer's wife. Knowledge is passed on by gradually initiating the youngster into all the arcana of farming, and the process necessarily involves the inculcation of specific norms and moral values, beliefs and habits. Both the content of this knowledge, which is the accumulated experience of past generations, and the mechanisms by which it is transmitted, attach great weight to tradition, and constitute the basis of the conservatism of the farmer's method of working.

In this system for transferring knowledge the school, at first, was a foreign element imposed from outside. It restricted the family's educational influence, wrested the child away from a harmonious system of labor and social life, and introduced into his mind patterns which were not in agreement with that system: foreign values, even values that could not possibly be realized within its bounds. Hence the opposition which this institution encountered and still encounters in the village today—an opposition which finds its minimal expression in the difficulties the village child has to overcome in combining learning and work.[1]

A closer look at rural schools will further clarify why they have faced so many problems through the years. But if the farmers did not think the schools helped their youngsters learn much about farming, they were aware of the fact that they directed attention away from farming to the more exciting milieu of the city.

RURAL SCHOOLS: PURPOSES AND PROBLEMS

The one-room school was the most common type of formal education in rural areas of America well into the twentieth century. Those settling the frontier established such a school as soon as practicable and kept it going out of local resources. In New England the small town was the unit of support, and this was duplicated with the settlement of what is now the Midwest. In the Southern states the county was the unit, being often larger than the town or township in other states. Since parents and governmental officials had to find the funds to maintain the school, through local taxation and at times through gifts, they took a great deal of interest in what went on there. The states had the right to create school districts and they provided some services and certain categories of support, but state authorities expected local government to use the property tax to pay for education.

1. Boguslaw Galeski, *Basic Concepts of Rural Sociology*, Manchester University Press, 1972, pp. 48–49.

The automobile and the improved road system made it possible to transport children from the inadequate one-room school, often located in the open country, to a larger school in a service center. Children could be graded in keeping with their age and ability, provided with more and better-trained teachers, given educational materials, and encouraged in diverse extracurricular activities, including athletics, especially in the upper grades.

During the period of consolidation, rural sociologists made many studies to determine the best social boundaries for the newly-created larger school districts; to describe the problem of parental and community control as education moved outside of the very small rural neighborhood. They were interested in the changed curricular content as well as the effect such schools had in eradicating the earlier differences in dress and manners between farm and village children.

One can talk about consolidation in the past tense. The number of school districts declined from 127,000 at their peak in 1932 to about 19,000 in 1970, with over 95 percent of this reduction being in rural areas. Yet, in 1966 there were still about 6,500 one-room schools in operation.[2]

Shifting the location of schooling to a village center did not mean the elimination of rural schools, for many of these consolidated schools were in agricultural areas where the village was simply a center for servicing the needs of farmers. Such schools, though in many ways superior to one-room schools, were still disadvantaged in comparison with most of the better-financed urban schools. Rural values still were important and many of the pupils expected to continue with farming, though the proportion declined with the changing economic requirements of agriculture.

Predominantly rural school districts in many states are joining together in some program of regional education. This can be done through merging of consolidated districts into even larger units, or it can be accomplished by setting up regional educational service agencies which help school districts with a wide variety of problems. Each year more states pass enabling legislation to encourage the regional approach, which seems to be the best answer yet devised to the handicaps of the school district that is too small and too poorly financed to give its pupils the kind of education they deserve.[3]

School systems outside the United States represent a wide variety of structures and problems. The rural schools in developing countries face many of the same problems that the United States experienced in its development, though always in a different cultural context. Such issues

2. Burton W. Kreitlow, "Rural Education: Overview," *The Encyclopedia of Education*, Vol. 7, New York: Macmillan and the Free Press, 1971, p. 576.

3. E. Robert Stephens, "Rural Education: Regional Approach to Programs," *The Encyclopedia of Education, ibid.*, pp. 583–89.

include a pupil-teacher ratio resulting in inefficient expenditure of funds, a school term shorter than in urban areas, low teacher salaries, a need for the rural teacher to cover more subjects than the average urban teacher, inadequate physical facilities, rapid teacher turnover, narrow and limited curriculums that are often ill-suited to the needs of rural students, and lack of supplementary instructional materials and libraries.[4]

Rural schooling can also be seen in another dimension: namely, how it articulates rural children into the national traditions, as shown in Table 9-1. Unlike the United States, where control of education is decentralized, Thailand has a highly centralized system.

There are few nations whose public school systems are as centralized as Thailand's. All its teachers are employees of the nation. Each wears the khaki uniform required of all officials. His status is fixed by a civil service rank which has a precise equivalent in every other branch of government. A district officer can, in practice, call upon teachers to perform almost any government task. Every teacher in every village, no matter how remote, is under the authority of the national Ministry of Education. Salaries, promotions, educational policy, standards of instruction, textbooks, school budgets and examinations are all determined in Bangkok. This centralization makes for occasional inefficiencies. . . . Throughout Thailand, village teachers frequently complain that the standards and content of the curriculum are inappropriate to the children whom they teach. Thai public education occasions some local objections as the price of the overwhelming national unity of its organization.

The teacher lives much closer to the farmers than does any other official. His dependence on the state and commitment to it are far greater than any village headman's. The teacher is thus the ultimate contact between the government that begins in Bangkok and the common people of the most backward reaches of Thailand. In what he teaches, just as in his social position, he encourages the unity of national life.

The seminal symbols and substance of this national culture are also taught in school. Throughout the kingdom the curriculum is everywhere the same. It emphasizes the history of the Thai nation and the glory of its heroes; it teaches the geography and economy of Thailand. It clearly labels its morality and ethics as those of Thai Buddhism. As Civics and Government, the pupils are told about the Thai state and of their duty and loyalty to its officials and, above all, to its king. The small sons and daughters of peasants whose world barely reached beyond their village are awakened to the past splendors and future hopes of Thai civilization. Once a year, on Children's Day, the primary school pupils of Chiengkham entertain the townsmen. At one point, little Lao, Lue, Yuan and Shan—for these dialect groups compose more than 90 percent of the district's people—come on stage to sing, "Noi, noi, noi, noi, we are Thai children." It is more than an empty skit. Their parents may have few loyalties beyond the kindred, village and neighborhood. Those who have been to school know of a great nation and know that they are part of it.

4. T. Lynn Smith and Paul E. Zopf, Jr., *Principles of Inductive Rural Sociology,* Philadelphia: F. A. Davis, 1970, pp. 329–30.

In Thai primary schools, repetition and memorization are the styles of instruction. This is based perhaps on the Buddhist tradition of reverence for knowledge and also on the scarcity of textbooks and teachers. Walking by a primary school, one hears a score or more voices reciting a lesson. The lessons are standardized throughout the nation. On any given day in the school year one can, with only the slightest strain on his imagination, hear the sound of hundreds of thousands of childish voices chorusing in unison.[5]

An important function of rural schooling in many countries with numerous tribal groups or ethnic minorities is to teach a common language that has been recognized as the official tongue. The result is that in every village there is someone who can understand the language spoken in the national capital and an increasing number of people who can follow the radio and television broadcasts. This linguistic articulation is very important in a developing country.

Rural schooling has other effects. Just as it helps an individual improve his social and economic status, because of the increased qualification

Table 9-1   Rural Schools as Articulating Network

Statuses	Teachers usually from outside community; external certification; deviant role models.
Roles	Teachers conduct themselves as carriers of national traditions and culture; encourage promising pupils on to further education, usually outside community; may dress in ways different from local custom and even flout local conventions; compare local community unfavorably with larger communities; or, if interested in local people, may seek to introduce higher living standards (nutrition, hygiene, increased farm income) and enriched recreational programs (films, plays, patriotic celebrations, library); may take children on excursions.
Values	Textbooks and classroom discussions place much value on those in nonagricultural pursuits (political, military, scientific, educational, religious leaders); use illustrations featuring most modern settings; stress national rather than local values, "scientific" values rather than "wrong" ideas of parents.
Norms	School may replace local reward system (i.e., that which gives prestige) with national reward system; may punish behavior considered acceptable in informal groups but not in a formal school situation; may try to modify children's ideas of what is right and wrong, appropriate and inappropriate, permitted and not permitted.

5. Michael Moerman, "Western Culture and the Thai Way of Life," *Asia*, No. 1 (Spring 1964), pp. 44-45.

provided, so it helps a particular nation get greater recognition in the family of nations. Countries with low literacy rates, with low school-attainment rates, and with low newspaper circulation rates may feel that their low educational status reflects upon their nationhood. This is another reason why rural schooling takes on added importance.

A further argument for better rural schools lies in migration statistics. Under rapid urbanization, many rural migrants with poor educational background flock into the cities. Many cannot read, they have few qualifications other than manual labor, and their recreational patterns reflect this intellectual insularity. Such situations have brought about the governmental support for equalization funds, which guarantee every student—no matter how rural his school district may be—an adequate education. The failure to provide this schooling in a rural area works to the disadvantage of the city that later receives the rural migrant. Many states within the United States have for a long time had an equalization fund which redistributed to poorer rural counties sums for educational purposes over and above what these counties actually contributed in taxes. This helps eliminate a long-recognized unfairness: the burden carried solely by rural communities of educating large numbers of young people who will spend their productive years in urban settings and for whose education the city would not normally contribute unless there was some equalization provision.

There are, of course, students of rural education who argue that a unique type of schooling should be devised and administered specifically for rural young people; it will be different in many respects from that provided for urban students. These specialists argue that the supposition that all rural youngsters need an urban education is wrong and that the articulation of the rural population into a society is best achieved if there is a rural education program and an urban education program, both conveying the idea that each segment of the population is important for the overall welfare of the country. Apparently, the United States has passed the point of no return in such a debate, but many other countries have not. This causes them to inquire more fully into rural-urban educational differences.

RURAL-URBAN DIFFERENCES
IN EDUCATIONAL ATTAINMENT

Conflict theorists correctly call attention to built-in structural inequalities which keep the educational networks from functioning as true articulating mechanisms. Some people in a society have ready access to good educational opportunities; others do not. Allocation of resources may go disproportionately to the cities or even to certain social classes within the cities; those groups that are educationally deprived remain so generation after generation. Evidence of rural-urban differences in educational opportunity is not hard to find.

Educational levels are lower in rural than in urban areas. In 1970 in the United States, urban people averaged 12.2 years of schooling, rural nonfarm people 11.2 years, and rural farm people 10.7 years. The figures in 1960 were 11.1 for urban residents, 9.5 for the rural nonfarm, and 8.8 for the rural farm. But in some ways these figures are misleading since just as high a proportion of farm young people aged 16 and 17 are in school as are urban youth of the same age. However, well-educated farm youths leave the farm by the time they are 20 years of age, resulting in a population with less education than that received by the younger generation.[6] In the 1950–1960 decade, the lead of urban people over rural people in educational attainment widened rather than narrowed, but this trend was reversed in the 1960–1970 decade, as the figures above show.

Nevertheless, within rural society the nonfarm population is better educated than the farm population. Differences on the basis of income are also marked. One study of low-income Kentucky counties found that one-half of the youths with low social status had discontinued their formal education but only one-seventh of the youths with middle social status and one-eighth of the youths with high social status had done so.[7]

When one looks at educational attainment internationally, one finds marked discrepancies in many countries between rural and urban populations. In Brazil, for instance, only three children in rural areas for every 100 in urban areas completed five years of schooling. In the Philippines the proportion of children aged 7 to 13 attending school (1957) was 69 percent in the rural areas but 84 percent in the urban areas.[8]

The factors accounting for these discrepancies are well known. One is the attitude of parents toward the value of education for their children. Especially in agriculture, children's labor can make a contribution, a fact which parents weigh against the value of the kind of schooling offered in their rural community. Child labor is still very common in a country such as Egypt where in 1960 about 10 percent of the boys under 15, and

6. Donald J. Bogue and Calvin L. Beale, "Recent Population Trends in the United States and their Causes," in James H. Copp (ed.), *Our Changing Rural Society: Perspectives and Trends.* Ames, Iowa: Iowa State University Press, 1964, p. 103.

7. E. Grant Youmans, "Factors in Educational Attainment," *Rural Sociology,* **24** (March 1959), pp. 21–28.

8. U.S. Department of Agriculture, Economic Research Service. *Changes in Agriculture in 26 Developing Nations: 1948 to 1963,* Foreign Agricultural Economic Report No. 27, Washington, D.C., 1965, p. 70.

11 percent of those aged 15–19 were in the labor force. With girls it was much higher for 37 percent of those under 15 and 14 percent of those aged 15–19 were actively working. About 90 percent of these young people were employed in agriculture.[9] In the United States as well, children of migratory agricultural laborers are employed in the fields. One investigation found that many parents choose this economic pursuit so that their children can be economically employed, thus improving the family income. They place greater emphasis upon the immediate earning power of their children than upon their long-range economic gains through education.[10]

Many studies show that young people on the farms have lower educational aspirations than the rural nonfarm youths in the United States,[11] but this need not be universally the case as a study in the state of Washington discovered. There aspirations had shifted to the point that 80 percent of the farm boys in contrast to 72 percent of the rural nonfarm boys wanted to attend college. In the opinion of the investigator, the reason for this may have been:

> The message concerning the need to leave farming has been heard and understood by the large majority of Washington farm boys and girls who are high school students. Those who plan to farm are evidently aware of the need for scientific knowledge as a basis for successful farming.[12]

In addition, the young people of Washington now see a college education as a favored channel to occupational success, in part attributable to the long-term influence of the state's educational systems, and in part to the mass media. Another positive influence on the educational aspirations of farm boys and girls was the peer group, particularly in the high school. Family background also played a part even though the parents of the farm young people were not as highly educated as those of the rural nonfarm young people.

9. Mostafa H. Nagi, "Child Labor in Rural Egypt," *Rural Sociology*, **37** (December 1972), pp. 623–27.

10. Frank A. Fasick, "Educational Retardation Among Children of Migratory Workers," *Rural Sociology*, **32** (December 1967), p. 402.

11. See A. O. Haller, "The Occupational Achievement Process of Farm-Reared Youth in Urban-Industrial Society," *Rural Sociology*, **25** (1960), pp. 321–33; A. O. Haller and Carole Ellis Wolff, "Personality Orientations of Farm, Village, and Urban Boys," *Rural Sociology*, **27** (1962), pp. 275–93; "A Note on 'Personality Orientations of Farm, Village, and Urban Boys'," *Rural Sociology*, **30** (1965), pp. 338–40; and Lee G. Burchinal (ed.), *Rural Youth in Crisis: Facts, Myths, and Social Change*, Washington, D.C.: U.S. Department of Health, Education and Welfare, Welfare Division, 1965. (Chapter 10 on "Educational and Occupational Perspectives of Farm and Rural Youth.")

12. Walter L. Slocum, "Reference Groups and Educational Aspirations of Rural Students," *Rural Sociology*, **32** (September 1967), p. 277.

To summarize, four major reasons for the rural-urban differentials in school attendance in the United States are:

1. The density of population is low, causing the special problem of social organization and transportation created by small numbers of people in large geographical space. . . .

2. The family-operated farm that involves a high labor input, both skilled and unskilled, can productively employ both boys and girls at a relatively young age. For those boys who want to drop out of school, productive employment is an alternative.

3. . . . Farming is understood by many as lacking the educational prerequisites of certain other occupations. . . .

4. Access to persons in a variety of occupations is not extensive in a familistic system limited to the same occupational group and style of life.[13]

For many countries in Asia, Africa, and Latin America, several factors have been cited as related to rural-urban educational differences, including some of those just listed above: sparsity of population, inadequate transportation, unwillingness of qualified teachers to live in rural areas, and reluctance of families to forego the assistance of children at home. Moreover, lack of facilities for secondary and higher education in many countries lessens the appreciation of even primary education.[14]

13. From Sloan R. Wayland, "Rural Education: Characteristics and Trends," Alvin L. Bertrand (ed.), *Rural Sociology: An Analysis of Contemporary Rural Life.* Copyright 1958 by McGraw-Hill, pp. 227–28. Used by permission of McGraw-Hill Book Company.

14. U.S. Department of Agriculture, *op. cit.*, p. 70.

CHAPTER 10
EDUCATION
AND
NATIONAL
DEVELOPMENT

Few people question the importance of formal education in a modern society. People who cannot read and write are at a serious disadvantage, and those without insights into how a society operates may find it difficult to pursue a career, or rear a family. There is an abiding faith that some useful purposes are accomplished by keeping children in school until their sixteenth year, but what these purposes are depend upon the school system itself and the expectations that parents and pupils have concerning it. Higher education has become a means of obtaining certification for many jobs that require this, even though the job itself may not actually need as much preparation as demanded in the job specifications. From the societal standpoint, the enrollment of a significant proportion of youths in schools beyond their sixteenth year keeps them off the labor market until a later period, thus lessening the difficulty of finding employment for those who seek work.

To say, however, that education is important in a modernized society does not explain whether or not education played a significant role in the modernization process itself.[1] In fact, students of social and

1. Vernon W. Ruttan, *Induced Technical and Institutional Change and the Future of Agriculture*, New York: Agricultural Development Council, ADC Reprint, December 1973, p. 5 concludes:
. . . the one inescapable implication of the results of our cross country analysis is the importance of literacy and schooling among agricultural producers and of technical and scientific education in the agricultural sciences.
Also see Guy Hunter, *Modernizing Peasant Societies: A Comparative Study in Asia and Africa*, New York: Oxford University Press, 1968. (Chapter X—Education.)

economic development still disagree on this matter. Those who argue the importance of heavy investment of resources in education by a developing country—changing from a rural to an urban society—do so by analogy from modern societies. Yet, this needs to be done with caution. One commentator points out that whereas sheer achievement of literacy is clearly a prerequisite to the evolution of any modern society, a nation of Ph.D.'s is not a necessary precondition. The question is not whether education is essential to development but rather what kinds, at what levels, in what quantities, how organized, and how administered.[2]

The historical role of education also seems clearer in countries that have modernized more recently (the Soviet Union and Japan) in contrast to countries such as Great Britain, which modernized much earlier.

Sometimes the consequences of schooling are not fully appreciated in advance. In India:

> Whoever gets educated today, irrespective of his social and cultural traditions and the economic circumstances of his family and community, acquires invariably the upper class prejudices and postures as well, the most outstanding of which . . . is a strict aversion to and disdain for manual work. He leaves agriculture altogether, because cultivation, or in fact any kind of manual work in the rural context, is considered totally incompatible with education. The result is that the spread of literacy among the peasant classes helps to improve neither the techniques of cultivation nor agricultural production—the two most pressing problems today in the agrarian field. Instead of being utilized to improve agriculture, education is looked upon as an avenue to escape from it.[3]

In other countries, such as those in Eastern Europe, the thrust toward industrialization has been stressed to the point that drawing people from the land to nonfarm jobs has been an active policy. In such a case, education which persuaded people to leave the farm had a positive rather than negative role to play in national economic goals.

The modernizing effect of education is also questioned by those who point out that education continues in most countries to be a "culture-preserving and culture-transmitting institution."

> Educational elites have been known to be guardians of the existing social orders more than innovators of the new ones. Whether on balance, the over-all effect of education is in the direction of modernity presumably depends upon (a) whether the educational system *is itself* being modernized,

2. Vincent MacD. Barnett, Jr., "The Role of Education in Economic Development," in Hobart W. Burns (ed.), *Education and the Development of Nations*, Syracuse, N.Y.: School of Education, Syracuse University, 1963. p. 16–17.

3. Kusum Nair, *Blossoms in the Dust: The Human Factor in Indian Development*, New York: Praeger, 1962, p. 149.

and (b) whether outside supportive influences exist that are conducive to individual modernity.[4]

These, then, are some of the points at issue in the debate about the role of education in development. These general considerations will become clearer if we look at two specific areas: basic skills gained in school, and the effect of education upon production of the personality type required in an industrial society.

Basic Skills Gained in School. The skill most often mentioned in any discussion of development is that of literacy. However, farmers often need to do simple arithmetical calculations. Often, arithmetic skills are included in the lessons provided in literacy programs, but arithmetic really goes far beyond the simple ability to read.

Many definitions of literacy have been contrived, the differences lying in the tests used to determine whether or not a person is literate. Rogers, in his study of Colombian peasants, defined functional literacy as "the ability to read and write word symbols at a level of competence adequate for carrying out the individual's functions in his social system." He measured this by asking each respondent to read a six-word sentence in Spanish. His findings, supported by similar results from India, were as follows:

> Functional literacy is related to mass media exposure (and even more strongly related to newspaper than to electronic media exposure); is more characteristic of children than adults; is associated with empathy, agricultural and home innovativeness, achievement motivation, farm size, trips to urban centers, political knowledge, and sociometric opinion leadership.[5]

In other words, his research indicates the importance of literacy as a variable in explaining many facets of modernization.

A study in Southern Brazil shows that neither lack of literacy nor of education make it impossible to reach farmers via the mass media. A small number of illiterates were even reached through printed media simply because they had someone around who could read the material to them. In fact, the number of illiterates reached through the medium of print was higher than those reached directly by the extension agents. The investigator did not conclude that mass media were a substitute for literacy,

4. Krishna Kumar, "Some Reflections on Individual Modernity," *Comparative Events* (Newsletter of the Institute for Comparative Sociology), 4 (Fall 1973), p. 4.

5. Everett M. Rogers with Lynne Svenning, *Modernization among Peasants: The Impact of Communication*, New York: Holt, Rinehart, & Winston, 1969, p. 92.

but did maintain that innovations among illiterates could be encouraged and influenced through mass media.[6]

Some studies of the social and economic effects of literacy argue that it affords an excellent index of the level of socio-economic development of a country. This argument is based on the grounds that behind the degree of literacy lies the whole institutional structure of society.[7] Further research, however, qualifies this by suggesting that the index of literacy seems to hold true up to a certain level of socio-economic development and after that either works in the opposite direction or becomes indiscriminating.[8]

One author also points out that universal literacy facilitates not merely peaceful reform, but it can help spread revolutionary movements that may prove disruptive to the development process as envisaged by the national leaders.[9]

The Individual and Modernity

Many who try to understand the process of economic development rely upon a theory of change that calls for personality modification in a sufficient number of individuals if the society is to move toward modernization. What interests us here is the part the educational system can play in strengthening the traits considered essential for the movement away from traditionalism to a nontraditional society. We will consider such traits as empathy, cosmopoliteness, achievement motivation, and then the syndrome of individual modernity.

Empathy. One of the major variables used by Daniel Lerner in his *The Passing of a Traditional Society* was empathy, or the ability of an individual to put himself in the place of another person, such as someone

6. John H. Fett, "Education, Literacy, Mass Media Exposure, and Farm Practice Adoption in Southern Brazil," *Rural Sociology*, 36 (September 1971), pp. 359–66. Also see Frederick C. Fliegel, "Literacy and Exposure to Instrumental Information among Farmers in Southern Brazil," *Rural Sociology*, 31 (March 1966), pp. 15–28.

7. Daniel Lerner, *The Passing of Traditional Society: Modernizing the Middle East.* New York: The Free Press, 1958. Also see Hilda Hertz Golden, "Literacy and Social Change in Underdeveloped Countries," *Rural Sociology*, 20 (March 1955), pp. 1–7.

8. David R. Kamerschen, "Literacy and Socioeconomic Development," *Rural Sociology*, 33 (June 1968), pp. 175–88.

9. Paul Fisher, "The Role of Education in Economic Development: A Response," in Hobart W. Burns (ed.), *Education and the Development of Nations*, Syracuse, N.Y.: School of Education, Syracuse University, 1963, p. 32.

living in the city or occupying a different social position.[10] That this is difficult for a traditional person to do was borne out in research before World War II in a peasant village in the Balkans conducted by the present author. A very conscientious, capable research assistant spent two days in the village trying to get respondents to answer a simple question: "If you were not a peasant, what would you rather be?" And the respondents were supposed to rank different nonagricultural occupations according to their preferences. At the end of two days, the research assistant gave up in hopeless despair because during that period of time he found no peasant who would answer the questionnaire. In every case, the conversation would run like this after the main question had been posed:

"But I am a peasant. I can't be any of those people."

"I know you are a peasant. But suppose you could be one of them, which would you rather be?"

"How could I be any of them? I don't have the education; I am only a poor farmer."

"But imagine that you were one of them. Which would you rather be?"

"A peasant is a peasant. He cannot be anything else."

And with that the conversation came to an end. Although the research effort was a failure, it nevertheless demonstrated in a spectacular way the inability of these rural people to imagine themselves in any status other than the one they held.

Lerner would hold that the ability to assume other positions, in one's imagination at least, is an important characteristic of the nontraditional person. This trait is positively associated with functional literacy, as Rogers has demonstrated in his study of Colombian peasants.[11] In another connection, Rogers points out that a person does not achieve functional literacy until after three years of schooling. After this point, he is able to continue learning from printed sources for the rest of his life. It is in the fourth or fifth grade that modernizing influences become probable "because (1) *course content* in postprimary classes is likely to reflect knowledge of a more modern sort; (2) the *location* of the post-primary school is usually in a town or city (rather than the local village), and the new environment is likely to have an urbanizing influence on the student; and (3) *teachers* in postprimary schools are better trained and more modern and, hence, provide their students with a personal model of more neoteric behavior."[12]

10. Daniel Lerner, *op. cit.*

11. Everett Rogers, *op. cit.*, p. 214.

12. *Ibid.*, pp. 78–79.

Cosmopoliteness. This is "the degree to which an individual is oriented outside his immediate social system."[13] Obviously it is related to empathy because the person with broad social contacts is more likely to "take the role of the other" in social interaction. The localite, in contrast to the cosmopolite, is concerned with his immediate environment. In the opinion of one social scientist Table 10–1 shows the antecedents, the initial external contact, the awareness of modern possibilities, the facilitaters of modernization, and the indicators of modernization.

The school can influence modernization by increasing the contact that the pupils have with the city, thus establishing a more cosmopolitan outlook. Trips and excursions to urban centers are illustrations of activities that might be carried along with the more frequent visits by urban people to the village classroom. Needless to say, media exposure of various sorts can promote greater familiarity with the city but, at times, it can have a negative effect in making the city seem less attractive, thereby decreasing cosmopoliteness.

Achievement Motivation. Hagen explains how economic growth begins by stressing the importance of such social values as achievement and autonomy in predisposing people toward accepting technological progress. These are learned in childhood.[14]

McClelland has also identified a popular need for achievement *(n* Achievement) as one of the two factors that have regularly preceded rapid economic growth. The second value he discovered in his research was "other-directedness," which he has described as follows:

> In societies which subsequently develop rapidly economically, the force which holds society together has shifted from tradition, particularly impersonal institutional tradition, to public opinion which helps define changing and functionally specific interpersonal relationships. . . .[15]

He views *n* Achievement as "a spontaneously expressed desire to do something well for its own sake rather than to gain power or love, recognition or profit."[16]

He cites three available means for bringing this about: the mass

---

13.   *Ibid.,* p. 147.

14.   Everett E. Hagen, *On the Theory of Social Change: How Economic Growth Begins,* Homewood, Ill.: Dorsey Press, 1962.

15.   David C. McClelland, *The Achieving Society.* Princeton, N.J.: Van Nostrand, 1961. p. 192.

16.   McClellan, "Changing Values for Progress," in Hobart W. Burns (ed.), *Education and the Development of Nations.* Syracuse, N.Y.: School of Education, Syracuse University, 1963. p. 63. Also see Bernard C. Rosen, "Industrialization, Personality and Social Mobility in Brazil," *Human Organization,* **30** (1971), pp. 137–48.

Table 10–1   Paradigm of the Hypothesized Sequential Role of Cosmopoliteness in the Modernization Process[a]

ANTECEDENTS	INITIAL EXTERNAL CONTACT[b]	AWARENESS OF MODERN POSSIBILITIES	FACILITATORS OF MODERNIZATION	INDICATORS OF MODERNIZATION
1. Proximity and accessibility to urban centers via (a) Roads (b) Communication channels	1. Contact with outsiders entering village	1. Awareness of new roles and opportunities	1. Higher aspirations (a) Educational (b) Occupational (c) Level of living	1. Increased Cosmopoliteness (a) Urban Trips (b) Mass Media Exposure (c) Change Agent Contact
2. Socio-economic facilitators (a) Status (b) Wealth (c) Leadership	2. Trips to urban centers	2. Awareness of the value of: (a) Literacy (b) Education	2. Acquire education and literacy	2. Knowledge-ability
3. Occupational facilitators (a) Teacher (b) Trader (c) Soldier	3. Mass media exposure		3. Seek new ways to improve income and level of living	3. Empathy
4. Personality factors (such as low dogmatism)	4. Residence outside the village (for example, military service)		4. Motivation to achieve	4. Innovativeness
				5. Reduced Fatalism

MAKE POSSIBLE → CAN CREATE → CAN MOTIVATE TO → WHICH CAN LEAD TO

[a]This is a hypothetical model which represents one way of looking at the modernization process, when the focus is upon cosmopoliteness. Within the limitations of our research methodology, we can offer only speculations about the time-order sequence of the variables involved in modernization. While we cannot *prove* the validity of the notions implied in our cosmopoliteness paradigm, we can support our contentions with logical reasoning and evidence from correlational research, as well as data from observational studies. The relationships we hypothesize are possible and probable, but represent only one arbitrary view of the concepts that are discussed.

[b]This initial contact may lead to further cosmopoliteness (as indicated, in the paradigm) or cause a negative reaction to modernization. From Everett M. Rogers, *Modernization Among Peasants: The Impact of Communication*, New York, Copyright © 1969 by Holt, Rinehart, & Winston, p. 151. Reprinted by permission of Holt, Rinehart & Winston.

media, the political party organization, and the schools. Considering the schools he writes:

> Finally, the schools, themselves, provide an excellent opportunity for arousing a concern for individual and national achievement. Stories the children read in their textbooks can be changed so as to have an achievement angle, as they have been in Turkey.... Teachers, like party leaders, can be specially trained to develop a concern for the achievement of their pupils. Team sports and other competitive games can be promoted to train young people to work up enthusiasm for doing things well or better than others.[17]

Syndrome of Individual Modernity. One of the most ambitious research projects undertaken to date on the social and cultural aspects of economic development has been directed by Alex Inkeles. It is based on the results of a questionnaire administered in six developing countries: Argentina, Chile, India, Israel, Nigeria, and East Pakistan. Inkeles and his colleagues believe that there is "a set of personal qualities which reliably cohere as a syndrome and which identify a type of man who may validly be described as fitting a reasonable theoretical conception of the modern man."[18]

Inkeles found education the most important factor in moving people away from traditionalism toward modernity. He finds that for every additional year a person spent in school, he gains somewhere between two and three additional points on a scale of modernity scored from 0 to 100.

The effects of the school, according to Inkeles, reside not mainly in its formal, explicit, self-conscious pedagogic activity, but in the fact that a school is an *organization*. In learning to deal with the school as an organization, pupils learn much about dealing with other aspects of society which also are organized. The factory, too, serves as a school and thus along with formal education makes a major contribution toward the creation of the modern person.[19]

Education, however, must be seen in broader terms than the formal schooling of the children and young people. Many educational programs exist for adults as well.

---

17. *Ibid.*, pp. 68–69.

18. Alex Inkeles, "Making Men Modern: On the Causes and Consequences of Individual Change in Six Developing Countries," *The American Journal of Sociology,* **75** (September 1969), p. 210. (For full study see Alex Inkeles and David H. Smith, *Becoming Modern: Individual Change in Six Developing Countries,* Cambridge, Mass.: Harvard University Press, 1974.)

19. For a critique of this approach to modernity see Michael Armer and Allan Schnaiberg, "Measuring Individual Modernity," *American Sociological Review,* **37** (1972), pp. 301–16.

ADULT EDUCATION AND THE DIFFUSION
OF FARM AND HOME PRACTICES

An example of a large-scale adult educational program is the United States Cooperative Extension Service in Agriculture and Home Economics. It came into existence in 1914 by an act of Congress, known as the Smith-Lever Act. The timing was propitious. Not only had agricultural colleges been established in every state as a result of the Morrill Act of 1862, but World War I placed a great demand upon United States agriculture, leading to expansion of farm acreage and to heightened efficiency. Through the years, the Extension Service has been credited with playing an important role in the success story of American agriculture.

As Figure 10–1 shows, the Extension Service is cooperative in that it involves the county, state, and federal levels of government. People at the county level have a say in selecting their own county agent, the home demonstration agent, and the 4-H Club Agent. The state becomes involved since these extension agents are employees of the state land grant university, an arrangement highlighting the educational feature of this program. Unlike the agricultural advisory services in many other countries, these agents are not connected exclusively with an administrative agency that uses them as an arm of the state to carry out what may at times be unpopular agriculture policies. Although the extension personnel from time to time have had some responsibilities for national farm programs, their function has remained primarily educational.

At the state college of agriculture, there exist subject-matter specialists (horticulture, dairying, nutrition, etc.) who serve as resource people for the county agent and his staff, who are generalists. This means that if a farmer brings in a problem that the county agent is not equipped to handle, the agent can immediately get valid information from the appropriate subject-matter specialist. These specialists, in turn, are in close contact with the research specialists in the agricultural experiment station, also located at the college of agriculture, so that any of their important findings can be relayed to the farm families through the extension personnel.

At the federal level, an office seeks ways of making the whole extension service more effective. It is in position to communicate to the states results of investigation by the various United States Department of Agriculture research facilities. One important facet of the federal office is the development of procedures for more effective training of extension personnel, though many of the efforts along this line are conducted at the state level.

In contrast to many other agricultural advisory services, most of the

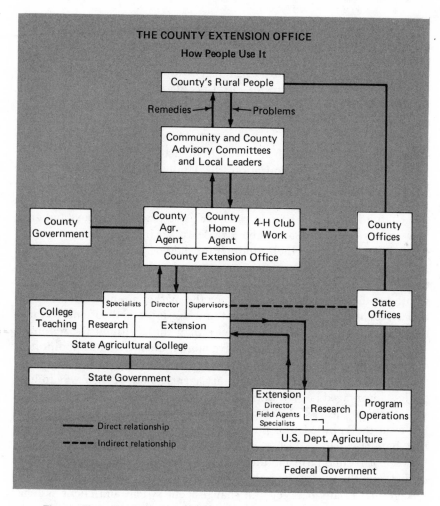

Figure 10–1 The organization of the Agricultural Extension Service. (From Arthur F. Raper and Martha J. Raper, *Guide to Agriculture, U.S.A.*, Washington: Agriculture Information Bulletin 30, U.S. Department of Agriculture, 1955.)

United States extension personnel have come from the farm. They have studied agriculture, and part of their responsibility is to show the farmer how to do things, even though it means the agent may have to "get his hands dirty" in the process.[20] In a number of other countries, the grad-

20. Francis C. Byrnes, "Some Missing Variables in Diffusion Research and Innovation Strategy," New York: Agricultural Development Council, Reprint, March 1968.

uates of the agricultural faculties are often urbanites who were not admitted into other branches of higher education and studied agriculture as a last resort in their effort to become a university student. They may know much about the theory of the agricultural sciences but are averse to actually demonstrating to the rural people how to treat a cow with a bloated stomach, or how to plant potatoes in a way different from the traditional practice. The rural people often sense a social and psychological distance between them and these agricultural officers and take a more skeptical attitude toward their advice than facts would justify.

With increasing urbanization, the United States Extension Service has sought ways to help suburban and urban populations and in some states is making significant contributions to these nonfarm people. The 4-H Club, which at one time worked exclusively with farm boys and girls, now enrolls city youngsters. The girls learn sewing and cooking, among other skills, and present their products for judging in county competitions.

One criticism of the extension service has been its failure at times to work sufficiently with the poorer farmers in the country. The farmers who have the resources to produce for the market are motivated to avail themselves of even more information and assistance and so tend to make much more use of the extension service than those without the resources. At times, the better-to-do farmers have more influence in the appointment of the county agent and his staff and expect more in return. But to counter this criticism of favoritism many county agents go out of their way to help the less advantaged farmer, but often with less favorable response.

Perhaps the less-advantaged farmers lack not only the motivation but even the knowledge of how to tie into the extension system should they be motivated. In fact, a study has been made of the systemic linkage between part-time farm families in a five-year extension program.[21] The study tested the general hypothesis that the greater the degree of systemic linkage that occurs between the change-agent system and client systems, the greater will be the changes occurring in client systems. This articulation came about as a new set of status-role relationships were established between the two professional people responsible for the program and the members of the cooperating families. Although the main purpose of the program was to aid in developing the resources of part-time families, a secondary result was the strengthening of the social articulation process by which families through an educational program became more closely connected with the larger society.

Sometimes extension workers find it hard to think of themselves as

---

21. J. Gilbert Hardee, "Planned Change and Systemic Linkage in a Five-Year Extension Program with Part-time Farm Families," *Rural Sociology*, **30** (March 1965), p. 26.

change agents, especially agents of change that goes beyond the technological innovation they seek to introduce. Yet they do conform to Rogers'
definition of a change agent as "a professional who influences innovation
decisions in a direction deemed desirable by a change agency."[22] Such a
professional essentially serves as a communication link between his clients
and the primary innovation source. "As such, the change agent is often
subject to role conflict because of his loyalty to two reference groups who
have different norms regarding change."[23] Therefore, his programs are
more likely to be successful if they fit the clients' cultural beliefs and values. Other factors of success include: involving clients in planning change,
increasing the clients' ability to evaluate innovations, and using opinion
leaders to spread the program.[24]

Different opinions about the effectiveness of the Extension Service
are based on varying criteria of evaluation. Without question it has been
a major factor in bringing agriculture in the United States up to its out-
standing level of production. Those, however, who would like to see it
become an agency for redistributing wealth from the richer to the poorer
farmers find it ill-equipped to perform this function.

Such considerations illustrate the great amount of attention given
by rural sociologists to the effectiveness of extension practices and to the
process by which new knowledge becomes known, accepted, and utilized—
all a part of the diffusion process.[25] This means identifying the channels
through which ideas and technology spread from the original center to
the farms of the nation. It calls for learning the characteristics of those
farmers most ready and those least ready to innovate. It means identifying
the stages through which the adoption process goes, as well as comparing
the relative merits of the use of media (radio, television) with the influ-

22.   Everett M. Rogers, op. cit., p. 193.

23.   Ibid., p. 193.

24.   Ibid., p. 194.

25.   See S. A. Rahim, Diffusion and Adoption of Agricultural Practices: A Study in
a Village of East Pakistan, Comilla: Pakistan Academy for Village Development,
Technical Publication Number 7, 1961; E. A. Wilkening, Joan Tully, and Hartley
Presser, "Communication and Acceptance of Recommended Farm Practices among
Dairy Farmers of Northern Victoria (Australia)," Rural Sociology, 27 (1962), pp.
16–197; Hartmut Albrecht, Theoretical Approaches of American Adoption Research,
Goettingen, Germany: Institute of Foreign Agriculture, University of Goettingen,
1965; Dario Menanteau-Horta, The Challenge for Change in Rural Chile: A Study
on Diffusion and Adoption of Agricultural Innovations, Agricultural Experiment
Station, University of Minnesota, Misc. Report 89, 1970; M. Cernea, Gh. Chepes,
E. Gheorghe, H. Ene, and M. Larionescu, "Socio-Economic Structures and Diffusion
of Innovation in the Rumanian Co-operative Village," Sociologia Ruralis, 11 (1971),
pp. 140–58.

ence of interpersonal relationships in persuading individuals to adopt a new practice.

Those responsible for adult education programs have made many efforts to use the various communication media effectively.[26] Studies dealing with the frequency of use become rapidly outdated as technological developments make it possible for even the most isolated rural people to use transistor radios.[27] Furthermore, television is becoming available to larger proportions of rural people throughout the world. An important finding seems to emerge from these studies of media in other countries as well as the United States: namely, the development of technology and the linkage of farmers to national markets or to central communication centers depends upon the degree of commercialized farming and the literacy level.[28]

It is also clear that radio and even television can inform rural people about many matters, but motivation is much more closely tied in with the opinion leaders, with interpersonal relations than with the media programs.[29] People in rural communities may see or hear a program designed to introduce change among rural people, or to educate them about some aspect of life (health, child care, better farming), but they hesitate to act on the program until they have talked it over with others in the community—with people whose judgment they trust.

A further finding is that people who have become accustomed to basing their decisions on information obtained from radio reports or from printed sources do so because they have found such reports useful. Where farming has not developed to the point that local activity is based on outside information, then the outside media seem much less important. Therefore, the media seem to carry out important articulation functions only when certain conditions have been met, the chief of which is the feeling that the information presented by the media is credible, that it can be trusted, and that it has applicability to the individual farmer's situation.

In conclusion, we might note that although we are gaining much

26. See Paul Spector et al., "Communication Media and Motivation in the Adoption of New Practices: An Experiment in Rural Ecuador," *Human Organization,* **30** (Spring 1971), pp. 39–46; John D. Early, "Education Via Radio Among Guatemalan Highland Maya," *Human Organization,* **32** (Fall 1973), pp. 221–29.

27. Everett M. Rogers, *op. cit.,* pp. 96–123.

28. M. Mohan Sawhney, "Farm Practice Adoption and the Use of Information Sources and Media in a Rural Community in India," *Rural Sociology,* **32** (September 1967), pp. 310–23.

29. D. T. Myren (ed.), *First Interamerican Research Symposium on the Role of Communications in Agricultural Development,* Mexico City, October 5–13, 1964. (163 pages.)

insight into the role of education in changing rural societies, we still do not have the kind of precise information that planners need. As pointed out earlier, we need more studies that do not deal with education as a broad concept but that investigate more specifically what kinds of education produce what results, at what levels, in what quantities, how organized and how administered. We also need further testing of the idea that "the effective 'starting point' for the transformation of traditional to modern social organization and behavior may be located within the personality systems of the participants in traditional societies rather than 'outside' of them—e.g., in the class structure of the society or in technological developments or in culture contact or in urbanization."[30] Most conflict theorists and some equilibrium theorists would tend to stress the factors outside of the personality of individual members. It would seem, however, that a mature sociology would recognize the need to move back and forth between the two resultants of human experience: personality and social structure. It could be really a matter of *both-and* rather than *either-or.*

---

30. Allan W. Eister, "Critical Factors in the Modernization Process in West Pakistan," *Year Book* of the American Philosophical Society, 1962, pp. 362–65.

CHAPTER 11
LOCAL GOVERNMENT AND POLITICALLY-CONSCIOUS RURAL ORGANIZATIONS

A key to the understanding of any rural society is the knowledge of local governmental structure and its operation. Akin to that is the way in which rural people become organized into large-scale organizations and associations in order to have greater influence in the national society, often in terms of governmental policies.

LOCAL GOVERNMENT

The original and smallest unit of local government in the United States is the *town,* which is found in the six New England states. The *township,* which occurs in 16 states, is, like the town, a definite community or locality group characterized by personal relations between citizens and officials. The *incorporated village* arises because people want control over the maintenance of public improvements instead of depending upon a larger unit of government such as the county. The *county,* in turn, is the prevalent form of local government for rural people since it is widespread throughout the United States and contrasts with *municipalities,* which by definition are usually urban and not rural.[1] In their analysis of the county as a social system, Loomis and Beegle emphasize its community character in that local people want to keep the conduct of public services under their scrutiny. For this rea-

---

1. Dwight Sanderson, *Rural Sociology and Rural Social Organization,* New York: John Wiley & Sons, 1942, Chap. 19.

son, the members of the governing boards have been predominantly farmers and a few businessmen and retired persons, with people of high social rank seldom represented. Election to county office is less dependent upon technical competence than upon knowing the right people. In other words, universalistic norms and procedures are uncommon.[2]

Other forms of local government are *special districts* for water, electricity, fire, education, roads, soil conservation, sewage, and the like.

Figure 11–1 indicates some of the statuses in county government whose incumbents play articulating roles between the rural people and the state and federal governments.

   1. Not all interaction between rural families and state networks goes through local (county) government.

   2. Familistic values/norms may link rural people with local governments; universalistic/contractual values/norms may tend to govern interaction with state networks.

   3. County officials often suggest proper roles that their constituents should play in dealing with external networks—a type of favor which helps keep local officials in power.

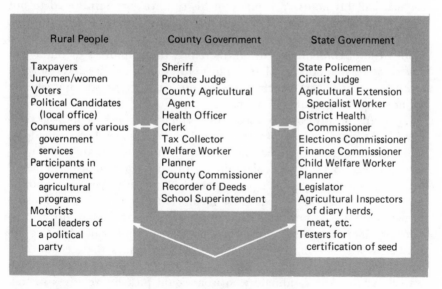

Rural People	County Government	State Government
Taxpayers	Sheriff	State Policemen
Jurymen/women	Probate Judge	Circuit Judge
Voters	County Agricultural	Agricultural Extension
Political Candidates	Agent	Specialist Worker
(local office)	Health Officer	District Health
Consumers of various	Clerk	Commissioner
government	Tax Collector	Elections Commissioner
services	Welfare Worker	Finance Commissioner
Participants in	Planner	Child Welfare Worker
government	County Commissioner	Planner
agricultural	Recorder of Deeds	Legislator
programs	School Superintendent	Agricultural Inspectors
Motorists		of diary herds,
Local leaders of		meat, etc.
a political		Testers for
party		certification of seed

Figure 11–1 Representative statuses in governmental articulation in the United States (each status stands for a specialized network consisting of a series of connected statuses).

   2. Charles P. Loomis and J. Allan Beegle, *Rural Sociology: The Strategy of Change*, Englewood Cliffs, N.J.: Prentice-Hall, 1957, Chap. 9.

4. Coercion lies behind taxing, licensing zoning for land use, school attendance, compliance with certain agricultural programs—e.g., crop reduction, sanitary standards in milk production and food handling.

5. For many United States farmers, policies and programs of federal government outweigh influence of state government as far as economic welfare is concerned, thus leading to "national" articulation.

In most of the world, local government does not have the autonomy found in the United States. Instead, it is simply an extension of the arm of central government and local people have little chance to control their own affairs. In Chile, for instance, the municipality is the unit of local government standing between the extensive networks of familistic relations that form the texture of Chilean society and the central authorities in Santiago, the capital of the country. Though these municipalities include urban as well as rural populations, their functions are strictly limited to collection of fees for licenses of various kinds. These fees provide insufficient municipal revenue with which local officials must cover the costs of collection and disposal of garbage, traffic control, street lighting, and public markets and gardens. Each municipality stands as the seat of government for the rural head of family who goes to its nearby center for many of his needs. Yet, many of his concerns are ministered to out of national offices in the distant national capital: housing, public utilities, street paving, education, health care, social welfare, and public security. With little of consequence to do, therefore, the employees of municipal governments are poorly paid and of low professional quality and restricted technical competence, which is the excuse cited by central bureaucrats for not entrusting them with more responsibility.[3]

In almost any country today, the *primary* network of local government is the group of local people selected to serve as members of the local administrative unit. Some families are represented; others are not. Therefore, families in the same community will differ in degree of influence over and benefits expected from members of the local governing board. Most of the time, they expect these members to favor their own kinship or neighborhood group since in a rural society interpersonal, direct relations are more important than the impersonal, impartial, objective approach to a situation. This explains why for decades the election of a county school superintendent in a rural Kentucky county has been such a lively affair. The candidate who won would pick his relatives to staff the schools, which were about the only places of steady employment in the county.

3. The material on Chile was adapted from John Friedmann, "The Spatial Organization of Power in the Development of Urban Systems," *Comparative Urban Research,* **1** (1972), pp. 5–42.

However, in changing rural societies today, local government is much more complex than the group of designated local individuals who serve it. In the United States as well as in the newly emerging nations, a cadre of professional or semi-professional people from outside move into the rural community to fill essential statuses.[4] The most obvious of these are the teachers, who may also be under the control of a school board, which is distinct from the governing council. Teachers look for enhanced status and promotion to the national ministry of education since, in most countries, the hierarchy of authority flows directly from the national capital, through a province or regional office, to the local school system. The United States is one of the very few countries where education is so fully a local affair; its hierarchy is discontinuous, with breaks coming at the local, state, and national levels. A measure of control is exercised through the funding procedures from the larger to smaller units. These outside funds provided for certain programs (school lunches, purchase of textbooks, etc.) are merely supplementary to the larger finances which local districts secure for themselves from local property taxes. Just as many smaller political units in the United States decided to consolidate elementary, junior high, or senior high school districts into central schools to which rural children were transported, so governments of other countries have selected central villages as the site of a larger school system to which boys and girls from the satellite villages belong.

Health officials, whether physicians, sanitarians, or public health nurses, are frequently a part of the local governmental network. Possessing considerable authority from the national ministry of health or state board of health, they must also work through a local Board of Health or the community council if they are to get the support and compliance of local people in their programs. Through the efforts of these health professionals, and with the approval of their fellow villagers comprising the governing board, rural people are offered, confronted with, or subjected to many practices that run counter to traditional folklore. By using a medicine prescribed by the local doctor to save the life of their child, instead of taking the child to a shrine for religious prayers and rites in accordance with rural custom, the parents subtly become linked to the modern scientific practices that characterize the emerging national value system.

Under certain conditions, the representative of law and order, whether a local constable, state trooper, or member of a national gendarmerie, can promote or deter the articulation of rural people into the national society. Deterrence occurs if his action in the name of the state is

4. See Arthur J. Vidich and Joseph Bensman, *Small Town in Mass Society: Class, Power and Religion in a Rural Community,* Princeton: Princeton University Press, 1958, Chap. 8.

so objectionable that people want to have less and less to do with the state he serves; promotion can occur if his dealing with people reveals a concern for their rights and their welfare. He may be the agent for distribution of relief supplies if there has been a catastrophe, or he may make his telephone available if it is the only one around, or he may be able to provide transportation in case of emergency. Whatever he does is done in the name of the government, local or national, whether the act be the unpopular arrest of a popular local person, the rounding up of draftees for the army, or the putting down of a group jeopardizing the peace and security of the community.

The examples of the outside professional or semiprofessional networks could be multiplied. This is because, accompanying any increase in highly specialized economic roles in a society, there is an increase in specialized governmental roles, manifested at the local level as well as in the highly developed centralized bureaucracies making up the government ministries.

Local government serves various interests through various networks: at times it seeks the action of the whole community, at times the support of a part of the community affected by some measure, at times the endorsement of a few influential local leaders. It is important to remember that the individual ruralite does not often make up his mind on any matter completely on his own, in isolation; he usually hears discussion about it not only over radio and television and in his family, but in his conversation with his neighbors, or at the chief community loafing place—coffee or tea house, tavern, or gas station.

While recognizing the important articulating function of local government, one must also be aware of the constraints it imposes upon individual actions. Joel Migdal has noted:

> Thus, even though the attributes of individuals for change may be present, change will not take place unless there are forces at hand which have weakened the village political community's capacity to restrain. It is then that one finds the fascinating phenomenon of individuals seeking a new polity in the large world outside the village, where men can change citizenship without changing their places of residence.[5]

NATIONAL ORGANIZATIONS
OF RURAL PEOPLE

Three types of large-scale organizations illustrate the changes occurring in rural society: the first is the agricultural cooperative which has

5. Joel Migdal, Research in Progress Note, *Peasant Studies Newsletter*, 1 (1972), p. 73.

already been discussed in Chapter 4; the second is the special interest farm organization; and the third is the national political party.

Special Interest Farm Organizations

Every country can provide numerous examples of farmers organizing themselves, or being organized, to gain benefits they would not obtain through individual efforts. Such organizations may lead to a major uprising or farmers' strike, others may turn into a political party, and still others may maintain a more limited objective of serving the rural people. The United States provides some interesting illustrations of farm organizations that have given rural people a greater sense of identity and at the same time have made them more fully aware of main currents in the national society.

The earliest of these was The Patrons of Husbandry, referred to as The Grange. Those who see Grange Halls in rural communities today are probably not aware that in the 1870's this organization had a membership of 750,000, comprised of people from every section of the country. It was designed as a fraternal, social, and economic organization with a secret ritual and with a hierarchy of officers who took their duties very seriously. Although not considered a political organization, it did lead a fight against the railroads, partly on the basis of what was considered unfair freight rates, with the result that government regulation of the railroads came into being. The members of The Grange cooperated in economic matters while their hall became a social center. The Grange officials also kept close watch on the voting records of state legislators and let them know in no uncertain terms what should be done to defend the interests of rural people. The influence of The Grange had declined by the turn of the century, but there has been a revitalization. Today The Grange has a membership of over 860,000 members in 37 states and stresses, among other things, the idea that the family farm is the backbone of American agriculture. It takes a stand on numerous national and international issues, thereby recognizing how closely its members are connected with concerns outside their own immediate communities.

Another important organization is the Farm Bureau, which came into existence with the Smith-Lever Act of 1914. This Act set up a system of county agricultural agents who were to pass on to farmers information from the state college of agriculture and the United States Department of Agriculture (see Chap. 10). One of the first things a county agent did was to organize a group called a Farm Bureau, composed of farmers who wished to improve their farm practices. In almost every county of the United States, such a local group exists and is linked with its State Farm Bureau Federation and with the group's national headquarters. Since the members are usually the better farmers of the community who have both the education and the resources for modern agriculture, their influence can be made to count with state and national officials. Though not a political organization, the Farm Bureau does represent its type of member very effectively. Since it also exists to help the farmer solve his various agricultural problems through the county agent, it links the farmer into the research networks of the state agricultural experiment stations and the bureaus of the United States Department of Agriculture.

Another organization is the Farmers' Union, founded in 1902 to help farmers, particularly in the South, to make a success of farming through a number of proposals regarding credit, marketing, education, and price policies. In its heydey it was considered a radical organization, a secret order, and tried to cooperate with labor. In the last few years it has grown more conservative in its program. The Farmers' Union has a membership of about 300,000 whose interests lie more in working family farms than in shifting to commercial farming.

These three organizations—The Patrons of Husbandry (The Grange), the Farm Bureau, and the Farmers' Union—illustrate the part such formal associations play in giving farmers a conception of their own importance, in publicizing their discontent, and in trying to influence legislators and others to take rural needs into account in a rapidly urbanizing society.

Arthur Mosher has pointed out important functions of farm organizations, whether cooperatives or special-interest types. Their first advantage is "that they can get tasks accomplished which individual farmers, acting alone, cannot achieve. And by involving group discussion of new ideas and *ad hoc* organization around a specific interest, they can affect the local climate of public opinion within which the individual farmer must live and work. In addition, they can shift the social organization of the locality away from groups based largely on birth, or on the needs of a largely static society, toward groups and prestige based on developmental activities."[6]

The National Political Party

The Grange and other groups (such as Farmers' Alliances) played an active role in the formation of The People's Party in the 1890's, which became known as the Populist Movement. One writer points out:

6. Arthur T. Mosher, "The Development Problems of Subsistence Farmers: A Preliminary Review," in Clifton R. Wharton, Jr. (ed.), *Subsistence Agriculture and Economic Development*, Chicago: Aldine Publishing Co., p. 10. Also see Darwin D. Solomon, "Characteristics of Local Organizations and Service Agencies Conducive to Development," *Sociologia Ruralis*, **12** (1972), pp. 334–360; O. Fals Borda, Cooperatives and Rural Development in Latin America: An *Analytic Report*, Vol. III,

... Economic conditions were quite favorable for the rise of a strong farmers' party at this time. Financial stress was wide-spread among the farm population. The prices of farm products were low, mortgages were being foreclosed on many farms, and the farmers were concerned about the causes of their financial distress.[7]

The party's first national convention was held at Omaha, Nebraska, July 2-5, 1892. The participants adopted a strong platform describing their grievances and nominated candidates for President and Vice-President, who received more than a million votes in the national election. In the next elections, 1896 and 1900, the party accepted William Jennings Bryan, the Democratic Party candidate, as its candidate, but he failed to win either election. From then on the fortunes of the People's Party declined.

But agrarianism did not die; it still persists, even though vast changes have occurred in the organization of American agriculture.[8] In order to measure agrarianism among Wisconsin Farmers, Flinn and Johnson specified five tenets of agrarianism that are embodied in Table 11-1. The respondents ranked 11 statements.

Tenet I, that farming is the basic occupation upon which all other occupations and economic pursuits depend, was strongly endorsed. Tenet II, that agricultural life is the natural life for human beings and is therefore good, was also strongly endorsed, but the other part that holds that the city life is artificial and evil was still believed in by the majority but not so strongly. Tenet III, that emphasized the importance of the economic independence of the farmer, held up with respect to avoiding debt but not very much with respect to disregard for cash income. Tenet IV, that the farmer works hard to demonstrate his virtue in his occupation, was still endorsed by the majority. And Tenet V, that the family farm is the backbone of American democracy, was also strongly agreed to by the majority.[9] When the authors analyzed what kinds of farmers were most agrarian in their views, they discovered that agrarianism was higher

Geneva: United Nations Research Institute for Social Development, 1971; M. J. McGrath (ed.), *Guidelines for Cooperatives in Developing Economies*, Madison: The International Cooperative Training Center, University of Wisconsin, 1969; K. Kamiya and D. E. Lindstrom, *Farmers' Organizations, their Role in Community Development in Japan*, Rome: Food and Agriculture Organization, 1967.

7. W. B. Bizzell, *The Green Rising: An Historical Survey of Agrarianism, with Special Reference to the Organized Efforts of the Farmers of the United States to Improve Their Economic and Social Status*, New York: Macmillan, 1926, p. 171.

8. Wayne C. Rohrer, "Agrarianism and the Social Organization of U.S. Agriculture: The Concomitance of Stability and Change," *Rural Sociology*, **35** (1970), pp. 5-14.

9. W. L. Flinn and D. E. Johnson, "Agrarianism Among Wisconsin Farmers," *Rural Sociology*, **39** (1974), pp. 187-204.

Table 11–1   Response of Wisconsin Farm Operators to Agrarianism Items

	STRONGLY AGREE	AGREE	NO OPINION	DISAGREE	STRONGLY DISAGREE
	.... (Percent)				
I. Farming is the basic occupation upon which all other occupations and economic pursuits depend.					
(1) Agriculture is the most basic occupation in our society and almost all other occupations depend on it.	83.8	11.1	2.0	2.7	.4
(2) A depression in agriculture is likely to cause a depression in the entire country.	73.1	17.2	3.0	4.0	2.7
II. Agricultural life is the natural life for man and is therefore good; city life is artificial and evil.					
(3) Farming involves understanding and working with the laws of nature; therefore, it is a much more natural occupation than others.	72.0	17.2	4.7	4.4	1.7
(4) One reason why we hear so much about crime and corruption today is because our nation is becoming so urbanized.	32.0	25.2	9.4	22.6	10.8
III. The complete economic independence of the farmer is desirable.					
(5) Farming should be an occupation where farmers are completely independent with respect to economic decisions.	23.2	24.6	6.1	33.7	12.4
(6) A farmer should be proud if he can say he owes money to no one.	57.6	18.9	2.3	12.8	8.4
(7) Farmers ought to appreciate farming as a good way of life and be less concerned about their cash income.	6.4	14.8	2.0	35.7	41.1

Table 11–1   (Continued)

	STRONGLY AGREE	AGREE	NO OPINION	DISAGREE	STRONGLY DISAGREE
IV. The farmer works hard to demonstrate his virtue in his occupation.					
(8) Farmers should raise all of the crops and livestock possible as long as there are hungry people.	45.1	26.6	4.0	18.2	6.1
(9) Lawlessness and lack of respect for authority are major problems in the United States today.	47.5	27.3	9.1	12.4	3.7
V. The family farm is the backbone of American democracy.					
(10) The replacement of family farms by large-scale farms using hired labor would have undesirable economic and social consequences for the nation.	65.7	16.2	7.7	8.1	2.3
(11) If the economic situation for farmers continues like it is now, in a few years the family farm will be replaced by large farms run by hired labor.	52.9	16.2	3.4	15.4	12.1

Source: W. L. Flinn and W. D. Johnson, "Agrarianism among Wisconsin Farmers," *Rural Sociology,* **39** (1974), pp. 196–197.

among farm operators who were relatively: (1) older, (2) less educated, (3) low income earners, (4) owners, (5) long-time farmers, (6) small-farm operators, (7) debt free, (8) seldom in contact with the extension agent or other agricultural college specialists, and (9) negative toward collective bargaining.[10]

Another work by Rohrer and Douglas has shown the continuing influence of agrarianism in a supposedly "modern" United States.[11] This

10. Ibid., pp. 198–99. In a subsequent article, F. H. Buttel and W. L. Flinn, "Sources and Consequences of Agrarian Values in American Society," *Rural Sociology,* **40** (1975), pp. 134–151 examine the data with reference to agrarianism among suburbanites as well as rural people in order to test which model (order-equilibrium or conflict) best describes the results. It was something of a draw, with a slight leaning toward the conflict model.

11. Wayne C. Rohrer and Louis H. Douglas, *The Agrarian Transition in America: Dualism and Change,* Indianapolis: Bobbs-Merrill, 1969.

indicates, as did the study of Wisconsin farm operators, that such values are associated with a lesser degree of articulation.

Accounts of agrarian parties in other countries show that each has its own characteristics related to the conditions faced by the rural people at the time. In describing the influence of national political organizations upon rural people, one must make an initial distinction between countries where two or more parties vie for power and those where a single party has a monopoly of power. In either case, the involvement of rural people in the political process may be considered important.

Two or More Parties

Each national party seeks to have its own representatives in as many communities as possible. Agrarian parties may succeed at this better than urban-oriented parties, but the goal of broad-based support still remains. If the rural community is large enough, local people serve as the chief spokesmen or committeemen for the various parties. Their duties are minimal, however. At election time they are notified that the candidate of their party will be speaking in the vicinity and are urged to drum up a good crowd in his behalf. They may also speak informally in favor of their party to anyone who will listen, repeating the promises the leaders will carry out in the event of victory. When the election is over, the local representative of the winning party may be called upon at times to intervene with party officials about the needs of individuals or even of the community itself: a new bridge, jobs in the government bureaucracy, or the replacement of the local doctor with someone more interested in his patients. As a rule, however, national political parties do not greatly affect the daily life of rural people—at least, as perceived by them. Campaigns do familiarize voters with the names and even personalities of the candidates so that the voters can follow newscasts of political events with more interest. Even the leaders of the agrarian parties are urban-oriented, frequently being lawyers who have managed to move into positions of influence in the party and who know how to operate within the national political arena.

A Single Party

Where a single party, whether politically left or right, holds a monopoly of power, it encourages *politicization*, or the penetration of its values and goals into every sphere of life. To see such a party at work one needs to understand its controls of the economy, education, its relation to the dominant religious institutions, its reformation of the family according to either traditional or quite new ideals, its concern for recreation in its control of content of media (including movies, telecasts, etc.) and in its structuring of local government. But even where there is a single party, much is frequently made of the election process. Whether there is a single slate of candidates or two rival slates approved by the central party officials, a campaign is held and all members are required to vote. All candidates, including the very top officials, run for office and carry on a vigorous speaking campaign throughout the district from which they seek election to the national parliament. This brings government to the people in the sense that it gives the hundreds of candidates an opportunity to present the major current issues as interpreted by the Party, thereby serving an educational purpose.

A one-party system is characterized, however, by much more than its legitimation through the election procedures. It also sets up a variety of mass organizations: for women, youth, members of various occupations or professions, and other interest groups. Some of these have been discussed in earlier sections, but they need to be seen here as part of the total impact that the national government tries to exert upon the rural sector. People are urged to attend, to participate, and to help implement any actions the group might decide upon, such as contributing four days without pay to harvest a crop for which labor is in short supply. The organizers of these formal associations come from outside, trained in group techniques, and try to raise the political consciousness of the rural people. Since both the organization and the content of the meetings often seem foreign or irrelevant to their interests, most local people attend only when facing sanctions for nonattendance, though a few see these organizations as a means for gaining recognition and perhaps a way to move into the nonrural sector of the society, either by becoming a party functionary or by getting a job in the city.

CHAPTER 12
THE NATIONAL GOVERNMENT AND RURAL SOCIAL CHANGE

Rural people throughout the world today increasingly look to national rather than local governments for remedies to their problems. This shift is in spite of the fact that there is traditional distrust of the central government by many rural people, that there is dissatisfaction with the reallocation of national resources among the various sectors of society, including the rural, and that there is reluctance to go into compulsory military service, where this is required. Each of these has some connection with rural social change as well as with the general process of social articulation.

THE RURAL PERSON'S DISTRUST OF NATIONAL GOVERNMENT

There are at least three reasons for rural distrust of centralized government, particularly in the old established societies of Europe and Asia.

First, the rural person who has not yet moved into the period of scientific agriculture does not feel the need of centralized government. It is outside his daily concerns. When pushed on this matter, he may grudgingly admit that some benefits flow from the government but that these do not outweigh its disadvantages. Such feelings, which may not actually fit the facts today, nevertheless have their roots in tradition. Robert T. Anderson in his study entitled *Traditional Europe* reminds us that in the past Europe consisted of three distinct cultures: aristocratic, burgher, and peasant.[1] The aristocrats were few in number but set most of the rules by which the peasants had to abide; the burghers were the city dwellers who followed a way of life very different from the rural villagers. The peasants' culture dealt with crops and animals and with a struggle to survive. Christianity was an important link tying the three classes together. The peasants would have recognized themselves to be a distinct group, if in fact they ever concerned themselves with such an idea, but they felt no responsibility for nor much interest in the details of whatever governmental units arose in the cities. In modern times, many rural groups still do not feel a part of the nation even though they may embody more of their nation's past than the national leaders.[2]

A second reason for the rural distrust of the central government goes beyond the mere feeling of distance from the seat of government to the very deep conviction that a government favors urban people and exists to exploit the rural population. Literature of rural life affords many illustrations of sons, husbands and fathers being drafted into the army to fight a war that had little meaning to the families involved. Rural people, including many who are already tied in closely to the national society, complain about and seek to avoid payment of taxes on their house, their land, their animals, and their crops. Folk traditions also are replete with anecdotes of ways in which some colorful villager tried to evade payment of taxes, even to the point of climbing a tree and staying there for two or three days until the tax collectors left the village after fruitlessly searching for him. In more recent times, where the national government fixes the prices of agricultural commodities or the interest rate on loans, the rural person may be convinced that he is being victimized. One of the most popular acts a new government can promulgate is a moratorium on all debts owed by the agriculturists to the state. By this one act, the government gains much approval from an otherwise disaffected element of the population. Of course, those farmers who had recently paid up their obligations would be distressed to think that less conscientious neighbors had gained a benefit over them.[3]

A third important reason for distrust of central government is the historical fact that it has frequently been controlled by foreign powers, whether in the tribal expansions in Asia and Europe or by the spread of

1. Robert T. Anderson, *Traditional Europe: A Study in Anthropology and History*, Belmont, California: Wadsworth, 1971.

2. Henry Habib Ayrout, *The Egyptian Peasant*, Boston: Beacon Press, 1963. First published in French in 1938. Translated by John Alden Williams.

3. This was in fact done by the "Colonels" who took over the government of Greece in 1967, but who are now out of power.

empires to neighboring countries and even across the seas to colonial holdings in Africa, Latin America, and much of Asia. The rulers, who did not speak the language of the rural people, required those of the native population who would deal with them to learn the imported language. In fact, many nations would not now exist if the rural folk had not resisted these alien influences and kept their own tongue and customs intact, with the result that when liberation came they constituted the bulk of the nation being recognized as a new and distinct political unit. But even toward their own government, which many rural people helped bring into existence, the farmers still show much of the inherited distrust which characterized their dealings with previous foreign governments.

In the New World, and especially in the United States, the farmers' skepticism about national government is not founded so much upon the factors prevalent in the old established societies. Rather, it stems from the ideology imported by the first European settlers who came to this country, with many of them making up its yeoman farmers. They, as well as the aristocratic gentlemen farmers, shared the idea set forth by John Locke: he who is least governed is the best governed. Consequently, the federal government was supposed to play as minimal a role as possible in daily life. Coupled with this belief was the emphasis in rural areas upon the values of hard work, independence, self-reliance, and "getting ahead." The opening of the West meant that new settlers (including many arriving European immigrants) moved farther away from centralized power and engaged in a pioneer endeavor matching their best efforts with the unfamiliar natural difficulties.

As a result of all of these factors, it is not surprising that national governments face an initial handicap in developing plans and programs for rural areas. Table 12–1 illustrates this in the case of two statuses.

Given this feeling of distrust and, at times, of outright dissatisfaction in rural areas, why are there not more rural uprisings? Of course, the historical record does reveal numerous examples of rural revolts, farmers' strikes, and peasant unrest. But these movements, which seek justice for the countryside, are usually short-lived. According to Eric Wolf, who has studied a number of such episodes, rural people may share a common vision but lack an organizational framework for action. "Peasant movements, like peasant coalitions, are unstable and shifting alignments of antagonistic and autonomous units, borne along only momentarily by a millenial dream." In some cases, such as the Russian revolution where "countries are so devastated by war that they experience a breakdown of traditonal leadership and social order" peasant discontent can be mobilized to fuel a revolutionary insurrection.[4]

---

4. Eric P. Wolf, *Peasants*, Englewood Cliffs, N.J.: Prentice-Hall, 1966, p. 108. Also see his *Peasant Wars of the Twentieth Century*, New York: Harper & Row, 1969.

Table 12–1   Rural Distrust of Government as an Inhibitor of Social Articulation

FARMER/PEASANT	GOVERNMENT OFFICIAL
Views official in terms of unfriendly stereotype.	Views farmer in a derogatory light.
Resists innovations suggested by official.	Becomes more interested in holding and advancing his position than in helping farmer.
Underrates value of services actually provided by government.	Seeks to have rural people bear more of the costs of development.
Seeks ways of circumventing governmental requirements.	Tends to rely more on coercion, actual and implied.
Develops solidarity of feeling with other farmers in opposition to official.	Accentuates class distinctions which set him off from farmer/peasant (e.g., let nails on little finger grow very long).
Familistic values emphasized over political values.	Appeals made in the name of the nation or national need.
Customary norms setting standard of behavior.	Invoking of statutory norms.

Result: Impasse

In their classic *Principles of Rural-Urban Sociology*, Sorokin and Zimmerman indicated that the majority of agricultural revolts are marked by a purely elemental, programless, objectiveless character. This is in contrast to urban revolts which show organization, unity, program, direction and leadership. Some of the farmer-peasant revolts have been directed against the city and its classes, sometimes upper and sometimes lower classes. According to these authors, the main cause of farmer-peasant revolts has always centered around land—its possession and redistribution. In fact, the radicalism of farmers has attempted to maintain wide distribution of private property whereas radicalism among wage earners has sought to concentrate ownership of property in the state or to do away with the institution of private property.[5] One implication of this relatively unorganized reaction or revolt of rural people is that no lasting social networks are set up through which articulation can be speeded up.

Increasing information about peasant movements and rural unrest comes from recent studies that seek to trace how peasants acquire power. On the basis of a study of Peru, Alberti proposes three general proposi-

5. Pitirim Sorokin and Carle C. Zimmerman, *Principles of Rural-Urban Sociology.* New York: Henry Holt, 1929, Chap. 19.

tions about the origins of peasant movements and their role in developing countries:

> 1. A peasant movement is the outcome of three interrelated social processes: (a) persistence of an exploitative relationship between landlord and peasant, (b) long range structural transformations that bring about loss of power of the *hacendado* (landlord) class, and (c) increased bargaining power on the part of the peasantry.
> 2. While the conditions create a structural situation conducive to peasant movements, precipitating factors must be present to serve as detonators... *the precipitating factors must not be taken as the cause of peasant movements.*
> 3. A peasant movement, when successful..., serves to remove the vestiges of archaic systems of production and the social relations associated with them. That is, it brings a "backward" social sector into line with the dominant mode of production and the social relations prevalent in a given region or country. In this sense, a successful peasant movement, from the point of view of deep national social change, can become a conservative force. ...[6]

THE RURAL SECTOR AND RESOURCE ALLOCATION

Rural discontent is based in part on the belief that the farmer does not receive his "fair share of the dollar." In other words, the nation's resources are not allocated sufficiently to the rural sector. How is such allocation carried out? One approach is the laissez-faire market system where supply and demand, through the price mechanism, determine who gets what and how much. At the other extreme is the centralized planning approach in which an official central-planning body determines the allocation of resources throughout the society. No country actually operates completely at one of these extremes, but each is usually nearer one pole than the other.

The Market

If a farm commodity is in excess supply, the price should fall so that more people will buy, thus reducing the excess and bringing about

6. Giorgio Alberti, "The Breakdown of Provincial Urban Power Structure and the Rise of Peasant Movements," *Sociologia Ruralis*, **12** (1972), p. 331. Also see H. A. Landsberger (ed.), *Latin American Peasant Movements*, Ithaca, N.Y.: Cornell University Press, 1969; A. Quijano Obregon, "Contemporary Peasant Movements," in S. M. Lipset and A. Solari (eds.), *Elites in Latin America*, New York: Oxford University Press, 1967; F. L. Tullis, *Lord and Peasant in Peru: A Paradigm of Political and Social Change*. Cambridge: Harvard University Press, 1970.

an equilibrium between supply and demand. Also, if the anticipated sale price of a given crop is low, farmers should produce it in smaller amounts, thereby creating a scarcity leading to higher prices when the crop is sold the following year. In today's world, however, production is only one factor; consumers expect the commodity to be processed, packaged and widely distributed, with the result that a larger share of the price paid by the consumer goes to the middleman instead of the farmer. Table 12–2 shows how the food basket is divided.

This table indicates that between August 1973 and August 1974 the retail cost of the fixed market basket had increased from $1,653 to $1,751, or a net change of $98. During this period the farmer's share shrank nearly 16 percent while the middleman's portion grew 29 percent. The table shows the components of the spread, with labor costs being the most prominent.

Therefore, through the market mechanism, money paid by consumers or buyers is redistributed to all of those who produce, process, and sell. Farmers do not get as large a share as they would like. Since they often form an important voting bloc, the central government in parliamentary societies abandons the strictly laissez-faire posture, where the market supposedly operates impersonally without government intervention, to guarantee base prices to farmers for selected agricultural commodities whose prices may otherwise fluctuate widely or whose production is considered essential to the economy. One of the best illustrations of a dramatic shift toward government intervention was the Agricultural Ad-

Table 12–2   How the Food Basket is Divided

	AUGUST 1973	AUGUST 1974	CHANGE
Retail value	$1,653	$1,751	+$98
Farm value	863	729	−134
Farm-retail spread	790	1,022	+232
Components of spread:			
Labor	387	501	+114
Packaging	96	124	+28
Transportation	58	75	+17
Business taxes*	32	41	+9
Other expenses	173	224	+51
Federal corp. income taxes	24	31	+7
After-tax profits of processors & distributors	20	26	+6

*Excludes federal income tax.
Source: Calculated from U.S.D.A. reports. From Monthly Economic Letter, First National City Bank, October 1974, p. 6.

justment Act, a major piece of New Deal legislation. Passed in 1933, and revised in 1938, it had the following goals:

> To conserve soil fertility by encouraging farmers to shift from soil-depleting to soil-building crops.
>
> To stabilize market supplies and prices of farm products so that there will be no surpluses and shortages to cause wide price fluctuations. For five major crops—cotton, corn, wheat, tobacco, and rice—the farmer is limited to acreage he can use, amounts he can market, and loans he can obtain for producing these crops.

The Act also recognized that farm purchasing power needs to be stable or else industry and commerce are adversely affected. Therefore, money was allocated to the farmer in ways such as these:

> 1. A farmer who keeps his acreage of soil-depleting crops within the prescribed amount is paid for this compliance.
>
> 2. Farmers can also earn extra payments for carrying out a "soil-building" program worked out especially for his farm. This might mean planting more legumes, trees, cultivating on a contour rather than up and down the slopes.
>
> 3. If the supply of a commodity is adequate to meet the demands of the market, the farmer can be given a loan to keep the commodity in storage, repaying the loan when the commodity is eventually sold.
>
> 4. Price-adjustments or parity payments are given the producers of the five crops mentioned above if the market price of any is less than 75 percent of the parity price (related to the exchange value of nonagricultural products for a given base-period).

The significance of this Act went far beyond its economic effects. It made almost every farmer in the United States eligible for some kind of payment from the federal government if he would comply with some of the provisions of the Act. But more than that, when he participated he automatically became a member of a County Agricultural Conservation Association, which administered the provisions of the Act locally through farmer committees. By 1938 there were 23,487 community committees of three farmers each, chosen by their neighbors to manage the program locally. Through such social groups farmers became connected with the county and state organizations and participated in decisions affecting their own welfare. This is a clear-cut example of articulation of the rural sector into the national society through a carefully-designed legislative act, where participation and compliance are rewarded by actual cash payments.

In the intervening years since 1938, many changes have been made in the provisions of the 1938 Act. World War II called for new efforts and new measures. The farmer in the United States was asked again to produce for much of the rest of the world and new programs were developed to gain his cooperation. By then, he was already an integral part of the economy, a businessman as well as a farmer. Furthermore, up to the present, periodic steps have been taken by the national government to maintain the purchasing power of the rural population.

Centralized Planning

In contrast to the idea of allocating resources on the basis of free market forces, some countries stress centralized planning. This assumes that the governmental leaders have set for themselves fairly clear-cut goals such as the number of bushels of wheat to be produced, television sets to be made, electronic engineers to be trained, fish to be caught, patients to be treated, new houses to be constructed, and so on through the whole set of products and services required for the total society. In addition, the planners have to determine priorities for a given planning period. They must decide whether or not a larger share of investment funds should go into industry than into agriculture, into urban rather than village improvement, or into social services rather than into enlarging the military establishment.

When such priorities have been set, estimates are made of the resources required to meet the top priority targets. These amounts are budgeted and set aside, with the remaining resources assigned to less important items in decreased amounts.

Such a system has its political and social flaws just as the free-market approach does. In most countries, especially in the newly-developing ones, planners, lacking accurate statistics, do not really know what resources they actually have and what combinations of them will produce stated results. As for agriculture, planners cannot control the weather and frequently find that climatic conditions or some farm pest or disease make them miss their targets by a wide margin. Since a country with centralized planning may have the same price for a given product everywhere in the country (be it a pair of shoes or a basket of apricots), rural people often lack the incentive to produce in quantity or to stress good quality. Many persuasive devices are used by the regime to enlist popular support in the fulfillment of the plans worked out by the central planning authorities.

In order to increase this support another approach, decentralized planning, has become widespread. Within certain guidelines set by the central authorities, people at all levels of society are asked to help determine the targets and ways of meeting these targets in their own factory, their farm, hospital, or economic enterprise. Therefore, the central authority delegates the specific decisions within the competence of particular groups to those groups, giving them thereby a sense of participation in the national plan.

The allocation of resources throughout a society is a much more complex process than the mere description of the polar types of the market and central planning would imply. As already indicated, the market today no longer operates without certain controls, many of which are directly related to the rural sector. And centralized planning is becoming democratized. Every step taken to control agriculture, to provide additional services for rural people, to force the shift of villagers into industrial centers, or to make farmers over into the image of the urbanite—through the use of public funds—has the effect of articulating rural people more closely with forces outside their localities.

This discussion of resource allocation again highlights the debate mentioned in the last chapter between those who stress the individual as the active unit of modernization and those who concentrate on the social structure. Where large numbers of rural people have unequal access to the "goods" of society, governmental remedies of some sort become the chosen vehicles for change (land eform, farmers' subsidies, agricultural development programs, etc.). This may mean, of course, changing the social structure if a whole class of people such as landlords are eliminated or greatly reduced in power.

THE ROLE OF THE MILITARY
IN SOCIAL ARTICULATION

Historians have noted the importance of military service in earlier time periods. Sabean, in studying market towns, notes these effects:

> Recruitment was centered in market towns in Southern Germany in the sixteenth century. Military enterprisers visited a town and recruited young men from the surrounding villages, who served as a unit for the season and then were demobilized to return to their homes. The network of relationships established in this way are important, for it was often by military service that a man built up a stake to buy a tenancy at home. As such men grew older and gained position in their villages they had a ready-made network of old ties that could be used for a variety of purposes. The part played by former soldiers in peasant revolts is well known.[7]

Rural areas even in more recent times have tended to contribute disproportionately to the military branches of their country. Military experience takes recruits out of the rural milieu to which they are accus-

---

7. David Sabean, "Peasant Society and Marketing Areas in Western Europe," Unpublished paper, 1973. Also see his "Markets, Uprising and Leadership in Peasant Societies: Western Europe 1381–1789," *Peasant Studies Newsletter*, **2** (July 1973), pp. 17–19.

tomed and puts them into contact with others whose home surroundings, while similar in many respects, may be quite different in others. Therefore, the first effect is to present the rural young man with a picture of life that is different from the one he has always tended to accept. He learns that villages in another part of the country have services and facilities totally lacking in his area. He learns that young people from another section do not ask their parents' permission before selecting a marriage partner. He finds out that agriculture is carried out quite differently elsewhere than on his own farm. This gives him much to think about. The travel he engages in as his military unit is moved from one location to another, frequently gives him a chance to talk to local people and reinforces this impression of alternative modes of life. He learns new values and becomes familiar with new norms.

A second well-documented effect of military life is the skills that it teaches. Young men unaccustomed to dealing with machines learn how to do so; others learn new methods of construction as amateur carpenters, stone masons, or iron-workers. Still others learn to cook and bake, serve as tailors, medical, or communications specialists. For some, learning to read is a skill newly-acquired in their military service. The recruit is thus prepared to play different roles as a farmer or to shift to another status altogether.

A third result of military life is the reinforcement of submission to authority, which was already a part of a patriarchal family system, but one in which a person heeded relatives, not strangers. Being placed, however, in a hierarchical structure based on division of labor and hierarchical responsibility rather than one based on age or kinship, is a new experience for many recruits. In a sense, therefore, it prepares one psychologically for roles in an industrial society where the foremen are not one's kinfolk and where fellow-workers do not come from one's own village with its particular orientation to the world. He thus learns how a social network, quite different from any that he has known, actually operates—at least from the soldier's point of view.

Few studies have followed up the behavior of those who go back to their village after serving their year, eighteen months, or two years in the army or navy. In general, it would be expected that they could apply only in limited ways what they learned. Only here and there could an innovation be successfully adapted. This fact alone might make the young man more prone to leave the rural community if he thought that a promising opportunity were available elsewhere. Although his ties may not have been cut by his months away, they may have been considerably stretched.

Very important, however, is the social mobility provided within the armed services themselves. Through demonstration of the proper qualities, a private might be promoted, thus starting a chain which could lead him to noncommissioned officer ranks. His chances of becoming a commissioned officer depend primarily upon entrance to a military academy, among whose cadets rural people are usually underrepresented despite the recent democratization of officers ranks in most countries.[8]

NATIONAL GOVERNMENT AND SOCIAL ARTICULATION

Norms of Coercion Versus Persuasion

It is very difficult for members of rural networks to interact effectively with external networks if the norms of the two networks differ greatly and are not understood or appreciated. There are certain urban structures, among them some government bureaucracies, whose rules and regulations are so drawn up that rural people may find it almost impossible to conform or qualify. This is a structural constraint. Furthermore, there may be such latitude given officials in playing their roles (carrying out their duties) that some of them may rely almost entirely on force rather than persuasion or education as a means of producing compliance. In looking at planned organizational change in traditional societies facing modernization, Jones lists types of strategies:

Coercive: Non-mutual goal setting and imbalanced power relationship. Rest upon application or the threat of application of physical sanctions, generation of frustration through restriction of movement or controlling through force the satisfaction of needs such as those of food, sex, and comfort.

Normative: Emphasizes normative power as a major source of control. Compliance rests primarily upon the internalization of directions accepted as proper and legitimate. The techniques of control are usually the manipulation of symbolic rewards, employment of leaders, manipulation of symbols, and administration of rituals.

Utilitarian: Characterized by control over material resources and rewards through the allocation of increased contributions, benefits, and services.

8. See H. Daalder, *The Role of the Military in the Emerging Countries*, The Hague: Mouton, 1969; John J. Johnson (ed.), *The Role of the Military in Underdeveloped Countries*, Princeton: Princeton University Press, 1962; Moshe Lissak, "Social Change, Mobilization and Exchange of Services Between the Military Establishment and the Civil Society: The Burmese Case," in Gayl D. Ness (ed.), *The Sociology of Economic Development: A Reader*, New York: Harper and Row, 1970, pp. 531–52; Jacques Van Doorn (ed.), *Armed Forces and Society: Sociological Essays*, The Hague: Mouton, 1968.

time. This depends upon, among other things, the effectiveness of meeting what people consider to be their important needs and upon the behavior of government representatives toward local people. This reaction can vary from time to time in a given locality as well as differ considerably from one place to another in the same region or country. Put in terms of our paradigm, to what extent is there growing mutual understanding concerning the statuses, roles, norms and values by members of the interacting local and national networks? Over and over again, administrators are admonished to respect the local culture as best they can, but far too often they do not even know what the local culture is.

3. A local government becomes less important as an articulating network when the society has reached "modernity" to the point that the average rural person is making more contacts with the larger society through nongovernmental channels, whether economic, recreational, the media, urban kin, religion, and the like. In such a setting, the national government is inclined to set up some programs which bypass the local government.

If we use Sub-Saharan Africa as a case in point, we note that governments there differ widely in their evaluation of the importance of local-central linkage. The governing elite in a country such as Tanzania places great faith upon microinstitutions that would mobilize the local subsistence farmer and his resources and would provide mass participation for people to discuss their local concerns. In French-speaking Africa, on the contrary, the prospects for developing effective political linkage networks between the center and local areas appear quite slim. Each level operates through different sets of institutions, with separate patterns of behavior, which perform separate functions. In such a case, social articulation is almost impossible. In the Ivory Coast, for instance, those at the center make little effort to penetrate the localities, preferring to let them remain firmly encapsulated units with considerable capacity to resist center penetration. In fact, some leaders maintain that national stability may best be obtained by encouraging local units to attend primarily to their own affairs, and that mass-participation may thus justifiably be discouraged. In fact, in French speaking Africa many of the elites do not think they need the mass support of the rural people since any danger to the governing elites comes from other elites, not the rural people. Other leaders suggest that at least limited center-local linkages might be important as a control tactic since local meetings held with senior officials on issues of local concern serve to identify possible opposition elements, who can be closely watched and, if necessary, suppressed. Micropolitical institutions developed for such purposes provide largely a one-way flow of information to the central government, assisting reelection and effective control. Some also maintain that as communication systems develop the

These are available to the client system when it performs in a manner ṗ scribed by the agent of change.[9]

All of these can be effective when used by government agenci under certain circumstances, but in the long run the normative strateg relying on participation and education/training, may be more propitiou for social articulation. Up to a point, conformity or obedience may b construed as articulation, but this may occur only at the level of role. (behavior) without internalization of norms or values.

Local-National Linkage

Distinctions need to be drawn between the part played by local governments and national governments in the articulation process. (For purposes of this discussion, state or provincial governments are not included though they too have a role.) One might argue in theory that the agencies of the national government provide the basic political networks through which rural people become linked with the national society. However, the degree to which they actually function in this capacity depends upon a number of situations:

1. A local government that provides comprehensive services in satisfying citizen needs, that is largely autonomous, where local people fill the major offices and familistic-communalistic values and norms prevail *may in reality serve as a buffer between the rural family and the central government.* In fact, it may refashion services provided nationally (education, health, welfare, law and order) in terms of local values and norms and thus foster a persisting parochialism, a feeling of "we" against "they," a traditional agrarianism. One might argue that the articulation of rural family networks into local government networks is a prior condition to linkage with national networks. Even if this should be true, most countries pursue a very different path.

2. A local government viewed as an arm of the national government may have few responsibilities delegated to it but may exist chiefly as a channel of communication and response between rural people and the central authority. The local government, in other words, is a place for outside agency representatives "to hang their hat" when they are relating to the local people. Whether or not social articulation is promoted will depend, of course, upon the climate of trust or distrust created through

9. Garth N. Jones, "Strategies and Tactics of Planned Organizational Change," *Human Organization*, **24** (1965), pp. 192–200. Reproduced by permission of The Society for Applied Anthropology. Also see Mario Barrera, *Modernization and Coercion*, Institute of International Studies, University of California, Berkeley, 1969.

masses become more aware of the real situation at the center and become more suspicious and hostile.[10]

These illustrations remind us that several patterns of local-national governmental relations are possible and each of them would have to be examined in terms of its own purposes and performance if its contribution to social articulation is to be correctly assessed.

10. This material on African local-central relations is taken from Michael Vickers, "Report and Commentary," on a Conference on Center-Local Relations and Political Linkage in Africa, held at Temple University, Philadelphia, Pa.

CHAPTER 13
THE RURAL COMMUNITY AND ITS EXTERNAL NETWORKS

The areas of articulation discussed in the preceding chapters represent some of the major institutional complexes which make up a society. They are functional units of the overall national social system. They exist in rural regions, though often in elementary form, as well as in urban or metropolitan regions. Therefore, to understand social articulation at the institutional level, we need to see how the rural family networks relate to urban networks, how the rural religious institutions articulate with the national religious structures, and how local government is a part of the national government.

Along with the institutional analysis, which deals with different major subsystems in turn, we also can view social articulation at the local community level. There the institutions (family, economy, education, etc.) are intertwined and interrelated in a fashion that may differ somewhat from community to community within the same society. This is because the members of a given community may readily accept some of the external opportunities or pressures and adapt to the network of which they are a part; or they may resist other external influences, since there is usually some element of choice. The local community is a mediating mechanism between the individual and the larger society;[1] it is often the "social world" of the relatively-isolated peasant, the place of residence and psychological identification for the farmer already geared in with national markets. The local community is where his

1. Edward Hassinger, "Social Relations Between Centralized and Local Social Systems," *Rural Sociology*, **26** (1961), pp. 354–364.

children are educated, where he worships, and where much of his informal social life occurs. Instead of looking at the articulation of the individual,[2] or the family, or the local government, we can analyze it in terms of ways in which the rural community is connected with the city.

THE RURAL COMMUNITY AND THE CITY

A number of social scientists have been interested in the unique factors creating rural-urban differences and similarities as well as in the process by which rural areas become more like urban areas (urbanization) or how cities are subjected to rural influences with the influx of many farm people in a relatively short period of time (peasantization of the city). Three approaches to this interesting question have been used: one stresses the differences, seemingly assuming a dichotomy between rural and urban areas; another approach uses the idea of a continuum, or the location of any given community somewhere between the two extremes of the traditional community and the cosmopolitan city; a third emphasizes not merely the continuum but the symbiotic or interdependent connection between the two.

The Dichotomous Approach

The rural community and the city can be viewed as two distinct ways of life that mix like oil and water. Those who hold this view often champion one against the other. They may be loyal agrarians who see in the countryside all of the virtues which have made the nation great or upon whom its future greatness depends; the city for them represents the downfall of man, his perversity, and his surrender of humane for materialistic values. They may be cosmopolitans who view rural areas as unsophisticated, illiterate, poverty-ridden, conservative populations who are so ground down by toil that they have no time (even if they had the inclinations) for cultured pursuits possible in the city. Furthermore they see each individual as so subject to local social control that he cannot be truly himself until he can enjoy the anonymity of the city. A review of the literature of almost any country will provide illustrations of these different points of view which divide the two ways of life to the point of considering one way good and the other bad. Value judgments come strongly into play.

2. J. C. van Es and J. E. Brown, Jr., "The Rural-Urban Variable Once More: Some Individual Level Observation," *Rural Sociology*, **39** (1974), pp. 373–391.

The Continuum Approach

Social scientists readily recognize that there are stages in between the extreme or polar types where actual social units would fall if classified according to the typological criteria. In this sense, the familistic-contractual and sacred-secular typologies may be viewed as continua.

One continuum that has had much influence upon students of rural life is the Gemeinschaft-Gesellschaft (Community-Society) of Ferdinand Tönnies, a German sociologist.

A key to Tönnies' system is the social relationship.

Tönnies assumes that all social relationships are created by human will. As social facts they exist only through the will of the individuals to associate. . . . A group or a relationship can be willed because those involved wish to attain through it a definite end and are willing to join hands for this purpose . . . In this case *rational* will, in which means and ends have been sharply differentiated, . . . prevails. On the other hand, people may associate themselves together, as friends do, because they think the relation valuable as an end in itself. In this case *natural* or integral will predominates. . . .

. . . There are degrees of rationality of natural will and of the communities and groups which it forms. Thus, in order of the importance of rationality there are the Gemeinschaft groups based on friendship, on neighborliness, and on blood relationships. Groups in which natural will predominates may range from those held together by intellectual ties to those bound by the instinctive liking or sympathy of biologically related individuals.

Thus, the businessman, scientist, person of authority, and the upper classes are relatively more conditioned by rational will than the peasant, the artist, and the common people, who are more conditioned by the natural will. . . .[3]

Tönnies identifies house, village, and town as representative of Gemeinschaft, with the town being the highest of these three. The city, on the other hand, is typical of Gesellschaft in general.[4]

Drawing up lists of characteristics of community and society is an idle exercise, however, unless such activity leads us to some understanding of social change. In viewing his polar type in terms of culture, Tönnies notes that a period of Gesellschaft follows a period of Gemeinschaft, with the latter characterized by "the social will as concord, folkways, mores, and religion; the Gesellschaft by the social will as convention, legislation, and public opinion."[5]

3. Ferdinand Tönnies, *Community and Society*, translated and edited by Charles P. Loomis, New York: Harper and Row, Harper Torchbacks, 1963, pp. 4–5.

4. *Ibid.*, p. 21.

5. *Ibid.*, p. 231.

According to Tönnies, villages develop into towns. Both of these have in common the principle of social organization in *space* instead of the principle of organization in *time* which predominates through the generations of the family, the tribe, and the people. In the village and town it is the physical, real soil, the permanent location, the visible land which creates the strongest ties and relations. In the period of Gemeinschaft, the younger principle of space remains bound to the older principle of time; in the period of Gesellschaft this becomes disconnected and from this disconnection the city results. The village, in contrast, remains essentially bound to both principles.[6]

It is clear that Tönnies is interested in drawing up major distinctions between the community and the urban-oriented society; he also looks for social principles operating in each type. He tries to describe the processes by which one type changes into the other type and in so doing he recognizes the existence of a continuum along which social units with various mixtures of the two polar types can be placed.

The Symbiotic Approach

To satisfactorily describe the emerging relationships between the rural community and the city we need to go beyond the dichotomy or even the continuum. We need to see how the two types join in a symbiotic relationship as part of a national society. Symbiosis is used here in the sense of a mutual interdependence brought about by the operation of impersonal ecological, economic, or other forces. Rather than seeing the village and the city as typological opposites or even viewing actual communities as closer to one type than the other, we need to concentrate upon their interrelationship in contemporary life.

One student of this phenomenon was Robert Redfield. He based his folk-urban continuum primarily on research done in Latin American communities. A distinguished anthropologist, he provided a useful distinction between the folk and urban society, describing in considerable detail the traits of a folk society.[7]

Basic to his approach are the concepts of *moral order* and *technical order*. He sees the moral order as binding together people through implicit convictions as to what is right, through explicit ideals, or through similarities of conscience. It is always based on what is peculiarly human —sentiments, morality, conscience—and arises in the groups where people are intimately associated with one another. It may exist in societies where

6. *Ibid.*, pp. 232–33.

7. Robert Redfield, "The Folk Society," *American Journal of Sociology*, **52** (January 1947), pp. 293–308.

rules for right conduct among human beings are supported by supernatural sanctions as well as in those societies where morality is independent of religion as belief and cult about the supernatural.[8]

The technical order includes all other forms of coordination that occur in human society. This order "results from mutual usefulness, from deliberate coercion, or from the mere utilization of the same means. In the technical order human beings are bound by things, or are themselves things. They are organized by necessity or expediency."[9]

Redfield observes that in folk societies the moral order predominates over the technical order, while in technologically developed civilizations the technical order becomes very great and relates to the moral order in varying and complex ways.[10] In contrast to the most primitive folk societies, the order of life in settled agricultural villages takes important account of the city. In fact, there were no peasants before the first cities and the relationship between the rural and urban poles are economic, political and moral.[11]

In the economic realm, the peasant has some product that the city consumes and relations are expressed in financial institutions; gain is calculated and taxation is present. But while dealing with the city, the peasant community maintains its local solidarity and makes institutionalized provision for the stranger (such as a money-lender) who can even live in the village but not be admitted fully into the moral life of the community.[12]

In the political sense, the city exerts power to control the local community in relation to the economic interdependence of peasant village and city, as well as through cultural advances such as entertainment and writing.[13]

As for the moral order, the peasant community and the city are closely related. "The necessary condition of peasant life is that the system of values of the peasant be consistent, in the main, with those of the city people who constitute, so to speak, its other dimension of existence. Peasants 'constitute part-societies and part-cultures.' "[14]

---

8. Robert Redfield, *The Primitive World and Its Transformations*, Ithaca, New York: Cornell University Press, 1953, pp. 20–21.

9. *Ibid.*, p. 21.

10. *Ibid.*, p. 24.

11. *Ibid.*, p. 31.

12. *Ibid.*, pp. 31–33.

13. *Ibid.*, pp. 34–35.

14. *Ibid.*, p. 40.

It may be repeated that the folk society is that society in which the technical order is subordinated within the moral order. The moral order is there, self-consistent and strong. As the technical order develops with the food-producing and urban revolutions, as the civilizations produce within themselves a differentiation of human types, and as they also reach out to affect distant peoples, there is a double tendency within the moral order. On the one hand, the old moral orders are shaken, perhaps destroyed. On the other, there is a rebuilding of moral orders on new levels.[15]

Thus, in summary, we have the two polar types: the folk society and the technologically-advantaged civilization. The settled agricultural community in contact with the city becomes a peasantry and is subjected to the dominant influences from the urban center, but the two remain dependent upon each other.

An excellent illustration of this interdependent, symbiotic relationship is the case of Neyl, a peasant village of the Lower Rhineland in Germany, and its relations with the city of Cologne.[16] In studying this village, Willems sought to test two ideas: one, that the peasantry was unable to preserve its cultural identity in the midst of "massive technological and economic change characteristic of the industrial revolution," and, two, the conceptualization of the relationship between peasantry and city in dichotomizing terms. He concludes that the residents of Neyl were able not only to survive within an industrial civilization without losing their cultural identity but were also able to use industrial wage-earning as a means of preserving the essentials of their peasant way of life. They became peasant workers. He furthermore found a cultural continuity between the urban lower class and the peasantry rather than cultural polarity between the two segments. In other words, a symbiotic relationship existed. The people of Neyl were able to assimilate changes imparted by the city and to reinterpret these changes in terms of their own values, thus seeming at first a unique case that runs counter to many studies of peasant communities. Yet, Willems thinks Neyl quite characteristic of peasant agriculture and society in certain regions of northwest Europe. This is explained in terms of a long-term historical process in which the peasantry of central and western Europe experienced an agrarian revolution that preceded the Industrial Revolution by several decades. The villagers provided food and labor to important networks within the city and in return received the chance to incorporate many urban amenities (modern plumbing and heating, for instance), while still holding to the agrar-

15. *Ibid.*, p. 48.

16. Emilio Willems, "Peasantry and City: Cultural Persistence and Change in Historical Perspective, A European Case," *American Anthropologist,* **72** (1970), pp. 528–44.

ian values of strong emotional attachment to land in the face of extremely rewarding alternatives to sell to the advancing forces of urban expansion and changing patterns of land use within the environs of Cologne.

Although many ideas have been dealt with in the discussion of the relationship between the rural community and the city, other ideas have been implicit. Some of these deserve further attention.

COMMUNAL ASPECTS
OF SOCIAL ARTICULATION

Though facing some problems, defining the boundaries of a rural community is a simpler task than trying to delineate an urban community. Thus, we can take it for granted that a rural community is a recognizable *locality social network* which in its own right can become articulated into the larger society. The most direct way it does this in a collective sense is through the local government but there are many other communal aspects of social articulation. First, we should distinguish between the indigenous, informal networks and those that are imported and formal.

Informal Networks and Social Control

The traditional networks in rural communities have tended to arise locally and represent response to important human needs. They are also informal in the sense that they are not *associations*, or organizations purposely brought into existence to serve a particular membership and usually with a set of designated officers or officials. (See Table 13–1.)

The informal networks illustrate Tönnies' concept of natural will, for they are deemed valuable as ends in themselves. The neighborhood is to be enjoyed and neighbors are not to be consciously "used" as would be the case in the rational will, where means are divorced from the ends—

Table 13–1   Examples of Social Networks in Rural Communities

INDIGENOUS AND INFORMAL	IMPORTED AND FORMAL
The neighborhood	The economic cooperative
The extended family	The mass political organization
Mutual aid groups	An adult education program
Religious, ceremonial groups	Community development program
Recreational groups	Youth sports group
	Local governmental council
	School board

such as a community development program. The extended family, too, is not formally set up to deal with a narrow range of problems as would be some city-based association, but it too is to be a source of security, emotional support, and a network in which much is shared. Mutual aid groups, including those involving work in the fields, are viewed as social occasions almost as much as work occasions. People are invited to participate because they enjoy being together and some unpopular troublemaker may not be invited, even though he or she might be a very good worker. Likewise the rural religious groups such as a congregation consider the weekly service or ceremony as an opportunity to meet with people as much as to worship and often resent the attempt by the religious leader to shift the focus from the Gemeinschaft character to a Gesellschaft in which the church program becomes all important and the informal visiting a secondary feature. Recreational groups, such as "women's gossiping groups" and men's tavern or teahouse cliques (where much gossip also flows) come together because those present derive satisfaction from being together. They are not trying to use each other for some ulterior end.

The above networks also illustrate Redfield's concept of the moral order since they are based on sentiments, morality, and conscience. The imported and formal associations tend to illustrate the technical order, although in many rural communities the moral order may appear even in the purposive groups, which are part of a regional or national body.

An important function played by the informal groups is the *evaluation* of the external networks. Within the community setting, people influence each other in determining how to cope with external networks. The evaluation takes place in terms of values, as the term would imply. What traditional beliefs and sentiments are called into question by the external network and how should public opinion be mobilized? Such public opinion is formed in the informal associations of which local residents are a part. Evaluation also takes place at the level of roles, or behavior. For instance, a Yugoslav textile factory posted a regulation that after a certain date all female workers were to come to work wearing slacks. This was at a time when slacks were tabu for the women in most of the villages represented. There was much discussion in the family circles, in the taverns, in the neighborhood work groups, but it was finally decided that the women had no choice but to conform. Since this was the general informal consensus no single individual who wore slacks felt very much censure from other women in the village.

Evaluation also relates to norms. The role had to do with whether the woman wore slacks or not, or her behavior; the norm had to do with the external regulation set by the factory. A rule may come from outside to the effect that all young people of a certain age must join a youth group, procure a uniform, and behave in prescribed ways. Is this rule to be enforced or not, or is it too foreign to local ways even to be considered? Or, a farmer with several horses may be told to bring them to a central market place for inspection by a veterinarian. Should he go to this trouble or not? Conversations with others in his informal groups help him decide whether to abide by the external norm or not.

Because there are these ready-made channels for communication and mobilization of opinion in a rural community, some types of articulation may take place much more quickly than if each individual, completely on his own and without benefit of influence of others, had to reach a decision.

Local Institutional Order and Its Disruption

One characteristic of a rural community already alluded to is the interrelationships among the local institutional networks. They form a web, as it were. The rapid social articulation of one institutional network into the national society affects its relationship with other local networks and may have repercussions for change much broader than originally envisioned or intended.

We can illustrate the effect of an external network upon a local community by a hypothetical case which Eberts presents. Suppose, for instance, one of the 200 largest corporations in the United States located a unit in a rural community, thus introducing a new linkage to the outside world. Some of the results, according to Eberts, might be the following:

There will be change in the patterns of communication within the community. Over time in a given community a pattern of communication between social positions (statuses) is developed, which, if it does not receive interference from outside forces such as new linkages, tends to become rather stable, or even rigidified, into a kind of equilibrium.

Certain subunits become much more powerful than other subunits, so that the more powerful subunits feel more free to communicate to the less powerful subunits, but the less powerful subunits are relatively cautious in the manner in which they return communications.

The appearance of a new linkage in a community tends to upset the previously established power relations. Especially when the new linkage is a large, important, and economically and politically powerful association like one of the 200 largest corporations, its appearance in a community will be a power with which the local power structure must contend by integrating it into the various aspects of community structure.

The changes in linkages will produce changes in the communication patterns of a given local community so that they will become more fluid, more open, as if they are between units which are more free and equal with each other.

If there is a lot of flow of information and resources in a given community then the fluidity among the local organizations will lead to 1) competition of ideas and resources, and 2) participation by the various subunits in the competitive political economic communication process of the community.[17]

Eberts then uses the concepts of competition and participation to draw up a typology of communities, each type of which has variations in the manner and degree of social articulation. The central point to be made here is that the local institutional order is disrupted and modified by the entrance of an external network, particularly if it can exert any influence or power in the local scene.

Increased Division of Labor

It can be posited that increased division of labor within the community will make social articulation more likely since the reference groups for many specialties will be networks outside rather than within the community. This applies to specialties in agriculture as well as within the artisan group and those rendering other economic services. Eberts notes:

> As differentiation increases in communities, certain more complex services require resources which go beyond the local community in order to find organizations which can more efficiently meet the needs of the local population. Thus, if people in a community come to need insurance protection, they usually must buy such protection from large firms outside the boundaries of their community. Or, when enough people need such protection, a large firm will establish an office, linkage, in the community to meet the need.[18]

One of Eberts' propositions is that to keep fluidity high in a community (exchange of information and resources), new linkages must be established. The reason is that otherwise the local institutional order would reestablish itself in an equilibrium that becomes less fluid.

A further effect of increased division of labor is that some members of the rural community may identify more closely with urban social strata than with strata in their own community. This can lead to social articulation within class networks which may have considerable political implications for the society at large.

The Problem of Local Autonomy

One of the recurring themes throughout the earlier chapters was that of local autonomy versus centralized national authority. Sometimes,

---

17.   Paul R. Eberts, *A Theoretical Perspective on Community Change and Development,* paper presented to the Association of Southern Agricultural Workers, Jacksonville, Florida, February 1971, pp. 4–6. Professor Eberts points out in a private communication that he has not fully tested the ideas set forth here.

18.   *Ibid.,* p. 9.

in reading accounts of social change, one gains the impression that rural people are helpless victims in an onslaught of external pressures; there are certainly cases where this could be the correct interpretation. But in the North American agrarian society, this does not seem to have been true. John W. Bennett has examined this matter, using three different rural groups in Saskatchewan Province of Canada. The first is the completely urbanized farmer who enthusiastically involves himself in politics and in the political struggle for natural resources and who stresses literacy and higher education for his children. A second is the rancher, who tends to avoid politics where possible, deals with external agencies at arm's length, preferring to manage his own enterprise in traditional ways. A third consists of Hutterian Brethren who completely withdraw from politics—local and national—and consider local cultural styles as alien; yet they are at the same time completely at home in the market economy of agriculture. Bennett concludes that in the mid-twentieth century the limitations of poorly developed transportation and communication have been overcome. Therefore, the incorporation of rural society into the national framework is close to completion. But he notes:

> ... the incorporative [articulating] tendencies in styles of life and economy do not necessarily mean that agrarian society is merely a suburb. Its agrarian basis means that it must continue to deal with agencies that are geographically and culturally distant, and that operate by rules differing considerably from those that may characterize the local social systems. In spite of the cultural and economic synthesis of rural and urban, there remains a pattern of interaction between microcosm and macrocosm, between agrarian world and industrial bureaucratic world.[19]

> The picture that emerges is more complex than the simplified one regretting the loss of "autonomy" or "independence." A more accurate understanding of the situation will recognize the existence of a process of adaptation in which the rural community is not necessarily at the mercy of the national bureaucracy, but in many instances manipulates it or evades its undesirable features.[20]

He reminds us that in North America today, the ruralite retains considerable scope for movement even as the agricultural economy becomes more closely tied to the national system. The farmer has wanted it this way; from the beginning of the settlement of North America his goal has been profitable commercialization. Even though not all farmers agree on the desirability of adaptive changes, they all recognize that they must find their way within this commercialized context. Furthermore,

19. John W. Bennett, "Microcosm-Macrocosm Relationships in North American Agrarian Society," *American Anthropologist*, **69** (1967), p. 443.

20. *Ibid.*, 452.

there is a continuing interplay between the local and the external and no single center of power dominates the entire society. So the characteristic interplay is a combination of autonomy and cultural distinctiveness with varying degrees of acceptance of externally derived frames.

As one looks elsewhere in the world, the picture is not always so favorable to the rural sector. In a colonial economy there is evidence of a growing gap between town and countryside.

> In a primary-based situation like Uganda or Tanzania the wealth of the country in terms of local revenue and foreign exchange is generated by millions of smallholders or plantation workers in the rural areas. Their produce is bulked up and exported through the main export point which is frequently also the capital city. The returning foreign exchange, which in the present dependency situation is seen as the engine of development, follows the same route in reverse and is creamed off in the cities. So those who do most to create the national wealth are at the bottom of the pile when it comes to handing out the benefits.[21]

In fact, in such countries the disparity between rich and poor takes on three forms: (a) the emergence and entrenchment of a small rich, capitalist class; (b) the accentuation of regional variations in wealth; and (c) the growing gap between the town and the countryside.[22] Under such conditions local autonomy is minimal; social articulation in the economic sense has outstripped all other forms of articulation to the point that there is serious social imbalance in education, social services, and other aspects of community life.

Network Varieties

All of the networks with which we have been dealing have the characteristic of being composed of social relationships, which in turn are made up of statuses, roles, values and norms. But some are general, others specialized; some are local, others are regional.

First, there are the institutional or functional networks that exist in rudimentary form in the village (except for the family) and in more highly elaborated forms in the larger society. The linkages between the rural and the urban representations of a given institutional complex constitute part of the social articulation process. Many formal associations are tied in with particular institutional networks.

Second, in contrast to these more specialized networks there are general networks such as the rural community. In most cases these can be

---

21. Randall Baker, "The Growing Gap Between Town and Countryside," *Rural Life* (England), **19** (1974), pp. 22–23.

22. *Ibid.*, p. 22.

looked at as sociological units engaging in decision making on certain issues, which exercise power vis-a-vis their residents, but which behave somewhat differently from each other when varying in social stratification, division of labor, size, homogeneity, and the like. Therefore, a community as a unit can be linked to external units through the articulating process.

Third, some regional networks can be identified either as specialized and administrative or as general and covering various broad areas of social life. These, of course, include communities as well as some of the institutional complexes representing the national society. One can then visualize social articulation as linking the regional networks into a greater whole.

SUGGESTED ADDITIONAL READINGS

CHAPTER 1

ADAMS, B. N. "Coercion and Consensus Theories: Some Unresolved Issues," *American Journal of Sociology*, 73 (1967), pp. 714–17.

BELLING, W. A. and G. O. TOTTEN (eds.). *Developing Nations: Quest for a Model.* New York: Van Nostrand Reinhold, 1970.

BERGER, B. *Societies in Change.* New York: Basic Books, 1971.

BERTRAND, ALVIN. *Social Organization.* Philadelphia, Pa.: F. A. Davis, 1972.

CHODAK, SZYMON. *Societal Development.* New York: Oxford University Press, 1973.

DAHRENDORF, R. *Class and Class Conflict in Industrial Societies.* Stanford: Stanford University Press, 1959.

DAHRENDORF, R. "Out of Utopia: Toward a Reorientation of Sociological Analysis," *American Journal of Sociology* 64 (1958), pp. 115–27.

EISENSTADT, S. N. *Modernization: Protest and Change.* Englewood Cliffs, N.J.: Prentice-Hall, 1966.

ETZIONI-HALEVY, EVA and A. ETZIONI. *Social Change,* 2nd ed. New York: Rinehart, 1973.

GALESKI, BOGUSLAW. "Conflict and Change as an Aspect of Development," *Sociologia Ruralis* 12 (1972), pp. 273–87.

GUSFIELD, J. R. "Tradition and Modernity: Misplaced Polarities in the Study of Social Change," *American Journal of Sociology* 72 (1967), pp. 351–62.

HALPERN, JOEL M. *The Changing Village Community.* Englewood Cliffs, N.J.: Prentice-Hall, Inc., 1967.

HARVEY, E. B. (ed.). *Perspectives on Modernization.* Toronto: University of Toronto Press, 1972.

HASSINGER, EDWARD. "Social Relations between Centralized and Local Social Systems," *Rural Sociology* 26 (December 1961), pp. 354–64.

HORTON, J. "Order and Conflict Theories of Social Problems as Competing Ideologies," *American Journal of Sociology* 73 (1967), pp. 701–13.

LAUER, R. H. *Perspectives on Social Change.* Boston: Allyn and Bacon, 1973.

LEAGANS, J. PAUL and CHARLES P. LOOMIS. *Behavioral Change in Agriculture.* Ithaca: Cornell University Press, 1971.

LENSKI, G. *Power and Privilege: A Theory of Social Stratification.* New York: McGraw-Hill, 1966.

LENSKI, G. and J. LENSKI. *Human Societies.* New York: McGraw-Hill, 1974.

MEADOWS, P. *The Many Faces of Change.* Cambridge: Schenkman, 1971.

ROGERS, E. M. and R. J. BURDGE. *Social Change in Rural Societies.* 2nd ed. Englewood Cliffs, N.J.: Prentice-Hall, Inc., 1972.

SMELSER, N. J. "Toward a Theory of Modernization," in *Social Change* by E. Etzioni-Halevy and A. Etzioni (2nd. ed.). New York: Rinehart, 1973.

SWANSON, G. E. *Social Change.* Glenview, Ill.: Scott, Foresman, 1971.

TAYLOR, LEE. *Urban-Rural Problems.* Belmont, Cal.: Dickenson Publishing Co., 1968.

TAYLOR, LEE and ARTHUR R. JONES, JR. *Rural Life and Urbanized Society.* New York: Oxford University Press, 1964.

VAN DEN BERGHE, P. "Dialectic and Functionalism: Toward a Theoretical Synthesis," *American Sociological Review* 28 (1963), pp. 695–705.

WALLERSTEIN, I. *The Modern World System.* New York: Academic Press, 1974.

WILBER, C. K. *The Political Economy of Development and Underdevelopment.* New York: Random House, 1973.

WISER, W. and WISER, C. *Behind Mud Walls, 1930–1960.* Berkeley: University of California Press, 1972 (Rev. ed.)

WOLF, ERIC. *Peasants.* Englewood Cliffs, N.J.: Prentice-Hall, Inc., 1966.

CHAPTER 2

MITCHELL, WILLIAM P. "Irrigation and Community in the Central Peruvian Highlands," *American Anthropologist* 78 (March 1976), pp. 25–44.

SHEILS, DEAN. "The Importance of Agriculture from the Perspective of Nonevolutionary Theory," *Rural Sociology* 37 (June 1972), pp. 167–88.

CHAPTER 3

GOLDKIND, VICTOR. "Sociocultural Contrasts in Rural and Urban Settlement Types in Costa Rica," *Rural Sociology* 26 (December 1961), pp. 365–80.

CHAPTER 4

BEAL, GEORGE et al. (eds.). *Sociological Perspectives of Domestic Development.* Ames: Iowa State University Press, 1971.

BENDIX, R. "Tradition and Modernity Reconsidered," *Comparative Studies of Society and History* 9 (1967), pp. 292–346.

BRINKMAN, G. L. (ed.). *The Development of Rural America.* Lincoln: University Press of Kansas, 1974.

GUSFIELD, J. R. "Tradition and Modernity: Misplaced Polarities in the Study of Social Change," *American Journal of Sociology* 72 (1967), pp. 351–62.

JONES, G. *Rural Life: Patterns and Processes.* London: Longman, 1974.

MINTZ, SIDNEY W. "Internal Market Systems as Mechanisms of Social Articulation," in Verne F. Ray (ed.) *Intermediate Societies, Social Mobility, and Communication.* Proceedings of the 1959 Annual Spring Meeting of the American Ethnological Society, pp. 20–30.

PATRICK, C. H. and RITCHEY, P. N. "Changes in Population and Employment as Processes in Regional Development, *Rural Sociology* 39 (Summer 1974). pp. 224–37.

SHANIN, T. *Peasants and Peasant Societies.* Middlesex: Penguin, 1971.

SMITH, T. LYNN. *Studies of the Great Rural Tap Roots of Urban Poverty.* New York: Carlton Press, 1974.

WHYTE, WILLIAM FOOTE. *Organizing for Agricultural Development: Human Aspects in the Utilization of Science and Technology.* New Brunswick, N.J.: Transaction, Inc., 1975.

ZIMMERMAN, C. C. and DUWORS, R. E. (eds.). *Sociology of Underdevelopment.* Toronto: Copp Clark Publishing Co., 1970.

CHAPTER 5

BERTRAND, A. L. and F. L. CORTY (eds.) *Rural Land Tenure in the United States.* Baton Rouge: Louisiana State University Press, 1962.

POWELL, JOHN DUNCAN. *Political Mobilization of the Venezuelan Peasant.* Cambridge: Harvard University Press, 1971.

ROSEBERRY, WILLIAM. "Rent, Differential, and the Development of Capitalism among Peasants," *American Anthropologist* 78 (March 1976), pp. 45–58.

TULLIS, F. LaMOND. *Lord and Peasant in Peru: A Paradigm of Political and Social Change.* Cambridge: Harvard University Press, 1970.

WILKIE, RAYMOND. *San Miguel: A Mexican Collective Ejido.* Stanford, Cal.: Stanford University Press, 1971.

YANG, MARTIN. *Socio-economic Results of Land Reform in Taiwan.* University of Hawaii, East-West Center Press, 1970.

CHAPTER 6

BRANDES, STANLEY H. *Migration, Kinship, and Community: Tradition and Transition in a Spanish Village.* New York: Academic Press, 1975.

LOOMIS, CHARLES P. et al. (eds.). *Turrialba: Social Systems and the Introduction of Change.* Glencoe, Ill.: The Free Press, 1953.

WILLIAMS, W. M. *A West Country Village: Ashworthy.* London: Routledge and Kegan Paul, 1963.

WYLIE, LAWRENCE. *Chanzeaux. A Village in Anjou.* Cambridge: Harvard University Press, 1966.

CHAPTER 7

MANGIN, WILLIAM (ed.). *Peasants in Cities: Readings in the Anthropology of Urbanization.* Boston: Houghton-Mifflin Co., 1970.

CHAPTER 10

CERNEA, M., GH. CHEPES, E. GHEORGHE, H. ENE and M. LARIONESCU. "Socio-economic Structures and Diffusion of Innovation in the Rumanian Co-operative Village," *Sociologia Ruralis* 11 (1971), pp. 140–58.

HERZOG, W. A., JR. "Literacy and Community Economic Development in Rural Brazil," *Rural Sociology* 38 (Fall, 1973), pp. 325–37.

KNOBLAUCH, H. C. et al. *State Agricultural Experiment Stations: A History of Research Policy and Procedures.* Washington, D.C.: U.S. Department of Agriculture, Misc. Pub. 904. 1962.

LOOMIS, CHARLES P. et al. (eds.). *Rural Social Systems and Adult Education.* East Lansing: Michigan State College Press, 1953.

MENANTEAU-HORTA, DARIO. *The Challenge for Change in Rural Chile: A Study of Diffusion and Adoption of Agricultural Innovations.* Agricultural Experiment Station, University of Wisconsin, Misc. Report 89, 1970.

SANDERS, H. et al. (eds.). *The Cooperative Extension Service.* Englewood Cliffs, N.J.: Prentice-Hall, Inc., 1966.

CHAPTER 11

LANDSBERGER, H. A. *Comparative Perspectives on Formal Organizations.* Boston: Little, Brown, Co. 1970.

MANGUM, FRED A. (ed.). *A Review of Agricultural Policy.* Agricultural Policy Institute, North Carolina State University, 1970.

SOLOMON, DARWIN D. "Characteristics of Local Organizations and Service Agencies Conducive to Development," *Sociologia Ruralis* 12 (1972), pp. 334–60.

CHAPTER 12

BEQIRAJ, MEHMET. *Peasantry in Revolution.* Cornell University, Center for International Studies, Research Paper V., 1966.

FIDEL, KENNETH (ed.). *Militarism in Developing Countries.* New Brunswick, N.J.: Transaction, Inc., 1975.

WILBER, C. K. *The Political Economy of Development and Underdevelopment.* New York: Random House, 1973.

CHAPTER 13

HEFFERNAN, WILLIAM D. "Sociological Dimensions of Agricultural Structures in the United States," *Sociologia Ruralis* 12 (1972), pp. 481–99.

WHEELER, W. "Social Change and Modernization: The Problem of Open vs. Closed Models," *Sociological Quarterly* 9 (1968), pp. 158–69.

INDEX